The HORROR *of the* PROFANATION *of the* MOST

Holy Eucharist

Rebel Priests who have the Blood of Christ on their Hands

MARK KREIS

Copyright © 2015 by Mark Kreis

The Horror of the Profanation of the Most Holy Eucharist
Rebel Priests who have the Blood of Christ on their Hands
by Mark Kreis

Printed in the United States of America.

ISBN 9781498429597

All rights reserved solely by the author. The author guarantees all contents are original and do not infringe upon the legal rights of any other person or work. No part of this book may be reproduced in any form without the permission of the author. The views expressed in this book are not necessarily those of the publisher.

Scripture quotations taken from the New King James Version (NKJV). Copyright © 1979, 1980, 1982 by Thomas Nelson, Inc. Used by permission. All rights reserved.

Scripture quotations taken from the New American Standard Bible (NASB). Copyright © 1960, 1962, 1963, 1968, 1971, 1972, 1973, 1975, 1977, 1995 by The Lockman Foundation. Used by permission. All rights reserved.

Scripture quotations taken from the New Revised Standard Version (NRSV). Copyright © 1989 the Division of Christian Education of the National Council of the Churches of Christ in the United States of America.

Scripture quotations taken from the New International Version (NIV). Copyright © 1973, 1978, 1984, 2011 by Biblica, Inc.™. Used by permission. All rights reserved.

Scripture quotations taken from the Interlinear NIV Hebrew-English Old Testament, Copyright © 1979, 1980, 1982, 1985, 1987 by the Zondervan Corporation. Used by permission. All rights reserved.

Scripture quotations taken from the Greek New Testament, Copyright © 1966, 1968, 1975, 1983 by the United Bible Societies. Used by permission. All rights reserved.

www.xulonpress.com

1) Consecrated girls / ST. J. Vianny — purchase 6 Bks
2) Fr. Dowdle
3) myself
4) Chaplain at Indiana school

This book is dedicated to my Beloved Mother Janina as a token of my gratitude for transmitted faith and love of our LORD Jesus Christ and His Holy Church.

I express my profound appreciation to all my Dearest Friends who supported me in finalizing the project of this book. My special thanks are addressed to my long-time mentor Reverend Charles Fanelli, Miss Louise Myszka for her proof-reading, Mrs. Mia Caroline and Mr. Jeffrey Banks for their technical support.

CONTENTS

FOREWORD ix
INTRODUCTION xix

PART I: An Epitome of the Teaching of the Catholic Church
        on the Most Holy Eucharist 23
1. The Mystery of the Incarnation of God. 25
2. The Presence of Jesus Christ in Every Part of the Eucharist 30
3. The Eucharist under the Form of the Consecrated Bread Alone. 40
4. The Salvific and Sanctifying Power of the Eucharist 49

PART II: The Profanation of the Sacrament of
        the Most Holy Eucharist in the Roman-Catholic Church 61
1. Sacrilegious Practices of the Profanation of the Eucharist 63
2. An Appeal to All Priests Who Profane the Eucharist 146
3. An Appeal to All Catholics of Good Will for Protection of the
    Sacrament of the Eucharist 175

BIBLIOGRAPHY 205

FOREWORD

The present book broaches the very urgent problem of the profanation of the Most Holy Eucharist, in the bosom of the Roman-Catholic Church, which spreads throughout North America as a pestilence. I have been compelled to write about this problem by my faith in the real presence of Jesus Christ in the Sacrament of Most Holy Communion, as well as by my irrepressible desire to prevent all Catholics from the demonic and sacrilegious practice of the desecration of the Eucharist.

The profanation of the Eucharist has become an enormous problem since the distribution of the Most Holy Communion under both species, that is, under the forms of Consecrated Bread and Wine, has unfortunately been introduced, and speaking more accurately, since the Eucharist under both kinds has willfully been forced by many liberal pastors and priests without a solid theological and liturgical preparation even before it was officially permitted by the Authorities of the Roman-Catholic Church. The problem consists in that after the distribution of Holy Communion under both forms, the remaining Eucharistic Blood of our LORD Jesus Christ is not immediately and entirely consumed during Holy Mass *before* the *Prayer After Communion*, but it is being carried away – usually by the extraordinary

Eucharistic ministers – to the sacristy of the church and poured into the sacrarium, that is, into a special sink which must have a pipe going directly into the ground. The sacrarium is used for washing the liturgical vessels or when the Blood of Christ is accidentally spilled out; then the area where the spill occurred must be washed with water, and the water which was used to clean the area with the Blood of Christ is poured into the sacrarium in the sacristy.[1] But the sacrarium is by no means designed to be a repository for the Most Precious Blood of Christ; in other words, the sacrarium is NOT a tabernacle!

However, this terrible crime has been going on for approximately a half century! It consumes the Mystical Body of the Church as a gangrene, and ruins the faith of many Catholics in the real presence of Jesus Christ in the Most Holy Eucharist, especially the faith of very many innocent children who serve in the Church as altar-boys and altar-girls.

The Most Holy Eucharist is being profaned by many priests, deacons and extraordinary Eucharistic ministers, but the weight of guilt rests, first of all, on the priests, and especially, on the pastors. It is the pastors and the priests who are above all responsible for the theological, spiritual and liturgical formation of the deacons and the extraordinary Eucharistic ministers, not vice versa. The vast majority of deacons and extraordinary Eucharistic ministers who pour the left-over Blood of Christ into the sacrarium do it because they have been wrongly trained by their priests. Therefore, the purpose of this book is not only to rebuke the priests who profane the Eucharist and teach others to do the same, but also to help all deacons and extraordinary Eucharistic ministers to become fully aware of the magnitude of the problem in question, as well as to realize how they have been

---

[1] Cf. *General Instruction of the Roman Missal* (Washington, D.C. 2003), p. 93.

abused and misled by those whom they should trust as their spiritual and liturgical leaders.

The priests, deacons and extraordinary Eucharistic ministers who profane the Eucharist can be divided into three categories. To the first one belong those who falsely believe that the pouring of the left-over Blood of Christ into the sacrarium is a legitimate practice of the Roman-Catholic Church. Their ignorance is due either to their intellectual negligence or to the wrong education which they have received at their seminaries and/or from their pastors at their parishes. The second group is formed by the priests, deacons and extraordinary Eucharistic ministers who are fully aware that the practice of pouring the left-over Blood of Christ into the sacrarium is strictly prohibited in the Church, but being intimidated by their pastors, they profane the Most Precious Blood of Christ. They "do not seek the Glory that comes from the only God" (John 5:44), "for they loved the glory of men more than the Glory of God" (John 12:43). They prefer to please their pastors, not God, and they do this to their own destruction. This is an obvious sign of their cowardice and disgrace. Finally, to the third and worst category belong the priests, most of them pastors, who actually know and are fully aware that the practice of pouring the left-over Blood of Christ into the sacrarium is unequivocally condemned by the Roman-Catholic Church, but nonetheless, with their diabolical defiance, they continue the profanation of the Most Holy Blood of Christ and force others to follow their evil practice. They are stiff-necked false shepherds in the flock of Jesus, who are extremely evil. They are more than common sinners; they are demons in human flesh.

The present book is primarily about those who form the last group of the most liberal, impertinent, disobedient and rebellious priests who continue their demonic activity in the very bosom of the Roman-Catholic Church, and who constantly have the Blood of Christ on their hands. However, the priests and deacons who belong to the aforementioned first two categories of those who profane the Eucharist are not completely excused, for if a priest and/ or a deacon does not know how he should deal with the Eucharist he should not be ordained, and if a priest and/ or a deacon does not have courage to defend the Eucharistic Jesus, he should step down, because the service at the Altar of Christ is not for cowards, but for those who are willing to mingle their blood with the Most Precious Blood of the LORD; they are to be faithful sacrificers, and not barbaric executioners who crucify Jesus over and over again. The hierarchical priesthood is not for those who want to live a comfortable life, but for those who want to sacrifice their lives for the sake of Christ.

In writing this book, I have drawn much inspiration from the Bible and the official texts of the Ecumenical Councils of the Catholic Church. I want to immediately inform the reader that if my language seems too harsh, it is often either the language of the Inspired Word of God, just as it is immortalized on the pages of the Sacred Scriptures, and/ or the language of the authoritative voice of the Catholic Church expressed in the texts handed down by the Fathers of the Ecumenical Councils. Writing about the profanation of the Eucharist, I could not find any better, more adequate and more appropriate language than the language of God Himself, continually speaking to us in and through the Inspired Words of the Holy Bible, as well as in and through the ecclesiastical documents of the Authorities of the Catholic Church.

The tone of this book is often exhortative, when I address the reader as if in a homily in order to stir up his conscience and simultaneously to impel him to action. Sometimes the Church can be renewed from above and sometimes from below. The faithful People of God must not leave the Authorities of the Church unaided. As we need the Authorities of the Church to guide us, so also the Authorities of the Church need us to support them with our *ardent, fervent* faith and *active* obedience. Everyone, regardless of his position in the Church, is morally obligated to take care of the Church, and everyone should do his best in contributing to the Church what is right in the Name of God, "for we are His workmanship, created in Christ Jesus for good works, which God prepared beforehand that we should walk in them" (Ephesians 2:10). Let us bear in mind that we are "fellow citizens with the saints and members of the household of God, having been built on the foundation of the Apostles and Prophets, Jesus Christ Himself being the chief cornerstone, in whom the whole building, being joined together, grows into a holy temple in the LORD, in whom [we] also are being built together for a dwelling place of God in the Spirit" (Ephesians 2:19–22), since we, "as living stones, are being built up as a spiritual house, a holy priesthood, to offer up spiritual sacrifices acceptable to God through Jesus Christ" (1 Peter 2:5). If our calling is so noble that we are – as Scripture itself testifies – "members of the household of God," "a holy temple in the LORD," "a dwelling place of God in the Spirit" and "living stones, being built up as a spiritual house, a holy priesthood, to offer up spiritual sacrifices," then it follows that we are also responsible for the Church as her living members. Therefore, let us spend ourselves in the service of our Mother Church by standing up against the profanation of the Most Holy Eucharist, and our sacrifice will surely be pleasing to the Heavenly Father, because everyone who defends His own Son in the Most Holy Eucharist offers a sacrifice which is acceptable to Him. Let us, then, sanctify Christ the LORD in our hearts, and always be ready to defend Him in the Sacrament of the Most Holy Eucharist (cf. 1 Peter 3:15), being armed with the power of God and the armor of truth in the right hand and in the left (cf. 1 Peter 4:1; 2 Corinthians 6:7) so that by them we may fight the good fight (cf. 1 Timothy 1:18) to the glory of God and the good of His Holy Church.

In the past, the Ecumenical Council of Trent (1545–1563) had to overcome the heretical teaching of those who had rebelled against the Catholic Teaching on the Sacrament of the Most Holy Eucharist, and at its Session 13, held on October 11, 1551, in the document, entitled: *Decree on postponement of the definition of four articles concerning the Sacrament of the Eucharist, and on the safe-conduct*, the Fathers of that council have written as follows: "The same holy council desires to uproot from the field of the LORD all the errors concerning this Most Holy Sacrament, which have sprouted forth like bramble bushes, and to provide for the salvation of all the faithful."[2] How much such a declaration is necessary today. The said council, in Chapter 8 of the *Decree on the Most Holy Sacrament of the Eucharist*, formulated at the same Session 13, has stated that "it is not enough to declare the truth unless errors are exposed and refuted."[3] This is exactly the prime intention and purpose of the present book. After many years of committing this horrific crime by so many Roman-Catholic priests in North America – who should be the first and the most zealous worshipers of the Most Holy Eucharist – it is time to speak bluntly about how they were and are totally, poisonously and deadly wrong in pouring the Most Holy Blood of Christ into the sacrarium. Holy Mother Church has entrusted

---

[2] N. P. Tanner, *Decrees of the Ecumenical Councils, vol. II* (London–Washington, D.C. 1990), p. 701.

[3] Ibid., p. 697.

her priests with the celebration of the Eucharist so as to nourish the People of God with the Living and Life-giving Body and Blood of Christ, but many of them act as though they were representing a step-mother or "a den of thieves" (Matthew 21:13; Mark 11:17; Luke 19:46; cf. John 2:16) who spiritually eviscerate and ravage the souls of believers, making them lukewarm or completely cold in their faith, by the manner in which they treat the Eucharistic Jesus, when they cast Him into the sacrarium. The Apostle Paul exhorts us in the following words: "Let a man so consider us, as servants of Christ and stewards of the mysteries of God. Moreover it is required in stewards that one be found faithful" (1 Corinthians 4:1–2). Those priests who profane the Eucharist prove themselves beyond any doubt as not being faithful servants of Christ, nor trustworthy stewards of the mysteries of God. On the contrary, they are acting as the enemies of Christ who crucify Him over and over again, and instead of being administrators of the Mysteries of God, they are rather the destroyers of the faith of those who believe in the Mystery of God revealed in the Sacrament of the Most Holy Eucharist.

When, on May 23, 1987, I was ordained to the priesthood, I would not have thought that in the years to come I would have to face this most grievous abuse of the Most Holy Communion which interiorly devastates today's Church. The profanation of the Eucharist prompted me to write my doctoral dissertation from the Biblical theology on the topic: *Symbolism of Offering the Pure Frankincense and Showbread (Leviticus 24:1–9)*. My doctorate is a kind of personal reparation for the profanation of the Most Holy Eucharist in which I show how, in the past, the sacrifice of pure frankincense and showbread, continually offered in the Meeting Tent, was the Old Testament *Proto*-Eucharist that was very profoundly cherished, as well as scrupulously and physically protected by the priests of the Old Covenant. None of the Old Testament sacrifices was so *Proto*-Eucharistic, in its nature and function, as the sacrifice of pure frankincense and showbread. It can be said that the Meeting Tent was the *Old Testament Upper Room* where the showbread was waiting for the Incarnate Son of God, the Divine Sacrificer and Victim, who is "the Bread of God" (John 6:33), "the Bread of Life" (John 6:35b.48.51a), "the True Bread from Heaven" (John 6:32b) "who [...] gives Life to the world" (John 6:33). From all the sacrifices of the Old Testament, be it bloody or unbloody, the sacrifice of pure frankincense and showbread was the only sacrifice which was *literally perpetual*, being offered "on the pure gold table before the LORD" (Leviticus 24:6; cf. Exodus 40:4a.22–23) twenty four hours a day, seven days a week. Every Sabbath Day, this liturgical bread of the Old Covenant was set out afresh, by the ministering priests, before the LORD (cf. Leviticus 24:8; 1 Chronicles 9:32). The sacrifice of pure frankincense and showbread was also the most protected sacrifice from among all the sacrifices of the Old Testament. It seems that the priests of the Old Covenant approached this sacrifice with a deeper devotion, piety and faith than many priests today approach the Eucharist, the True and Most Holy Body and Blood of our LORD Jesus Christ. If all the priests of the Roman-Catholic Church had so great a reverence for the Sacrifice of the Eucharist as the priests of the Old Covenant had had for the sacrifice of pure frankincense and showbread, which had only symbolized, foreshadowed and prefigured the Sacrament of the Most Holy Communion, then the profanation of the Eucharist would never have taken place in the bosom the Roman-Catholic Church.

On December 8, 1995, I wrote a letter to Joseph Cardinal Ratzinger, at that time Prefect of the Congregation for the Doctrine of the Faith, in which I beseeched him to put a stop to the profanation of the Eucharist in North America, but this crime is still going on in the Roman-Catholic Church, being committed with impunity by those who are appointed to guard this Most Blessed Sacrament. Almost 20 years have elapsed since the above-mentioned letter was sent to the Apostolic See. During this time, I have tried to intervene with the Ecclesiastic Authorities, but without any significant results. Therefore, I have decided to write this present book in order to break out in words of condemnation against this barbaric and cruel treatment of the Eucharistic Jesus; it is time to speak out and to remind all Catholics, not only in North America, of the morally death-bringing consequences which the profanation of the Eucharist entails. This is, indeed, a matter of life and death!

Lest there be any doubt regarding my intention in writing this book, let me make it very clear that it has been written at the dictate of my Christian conscience. I have determined to single out neither any personal name nor the name of any diocese. The intention is only one, namely, to bring to the attention of the clergy and the laity the problem of a criminal practice in the bosom of the Roman-Catholic Church which is thoroughly satanic in every sense of the word.

INTRODUCTION

There is a great need for re-evangelization of Catholics today, and not only Catholics, but Christians in general. As a matter of fact, if we want to be wise and faithful followers of Christ, we need to be re-educated over and over again. This pattern of constant re-learning is already contained in the Old Testament. Sacred Scripture relates that when Moses had written the Law, he "delivered it to the priests, the sons of Levi, who bore the ark of the covenant of the LORD, and to all the elders of Israel. And Moses commanded them, saying: 'At the end of every seven years, at the appointed time in the year of release, at the Feast of Tabernacles, when all Israel comes to appear before the LORD, your God, in the place which He chooses, you shall read this Law before all Israel in their hearing. Gather the people together, men and women and little ones, and the stranger who is within your gates, that they may hear and that they may learn to fear the LORD, your God, and carefully observe all the words of this Law, and that their children, who have not known it, may hear and learn to fear the LORD, your God, as long as you live in the land which you cross the Jordan to possess'" (Deuteronomy 31:9–13). Moses handed down the Torah to the leaders of the Chosen People which was to be read before all the Israelites at the end of every sabbatical year that they might hear the word of the LORD, and so to learn to fear their God, and to observe carefully all the ordinances of the Law. At the time of the Old Testament, every seventh year was for the priests, the elders and the entire People of Israel a very special year, the year of a great national education and re-education; it was a year of communal teaching and of learning the Law of God. This was an excellent practice which is so necessary today in the Church. As Israel of old crossed the waters of the Jordan River in order to inherit the promised land, so now we, the New Israel, have crossed the waters of Baptism in order to come into possession of the New Promised Land, which is today the Church of Jesus Christ. And as the religious life of ancient Israel was to be renewed intellectually and spiritually every seventh year by the public proclamation of the message of the Bible, so now we too need to read the Law of our LORD Jesus Christ over and over again that we may attend to His Divine Words that "are Spirit and Life" (John 6:63c), and thus to learn to fear Him and to observe carefully what He is teaching us through the Authorities of His Holy Church, the Church "that He has purchased with His own Blood" (Acts 20:28).

Unfortunately, there are some liberal priests who exhibit an *anti*-institutional and *anti*-doctrinal mentality, even to such an extent that some of them would *literally* prohibit making available the new Catechism of the Roman-Catholic Church in their parishes! They say that the content of the Catechism is too difficult for the people, and that they can be confused. In this manner, they insult the intelligence of their parishioners. Again, other priests claim that the people do not need to know the Catechism at all to be good Christians. No wonder that there are more and more Catholics who do not know their Catholic identity. The doctrine of the Roman-Catholic

Introduction

Church is not an intellectual threat to the People of God, but a beautiful ecclesiastic enlightenment which helps Catholics to be united in professing their common faith.

As an example, when the new English version of the Roman Missal was introduced, some priests complained about the terminology used in the new translation. The most criticized term is the word: "con–substantial"[4] which occurs in the *Creed*. I was at a meeting at which a priest said the following: "During Mass the people profess their faith and all of a sudden the word 'con–substantial' comes up, and they have no clue what this term is about." When I heard this comment, I could not believe that it was uttered by a priest. Every priest is morally obligated to teach the faithful, and this includes the explanation of the theological terminology which carries so profound a richness of its contents. The Bible reads that "wisdom is like her name; she is not readily perceived by many" (Sirach 6:22), and surely not by that poor priest who does not bear in mind that it is his sacred duty

---

[4] The word: "con-substantial" is the anglicized form of the Latin adjective: "con-substantialis" which stems from the Latin noun: "con-substatia." The term: "con-substatia" is built of the prefix: "cum" and the noun: "substantia." The preposition: "cum" (the old form of "cum" is: "com" or "con" as it occurs in compound terms, for example, our "con-substantial") means: "with," "together with," "along with." When the preposition: "cum" is used in the categories of *time*, it denotes: "simultaneously with," "at the same time with;" whereas the noun: "substantia" indicates: "substance," "essence," as well as: "means of subsistence," "property." And so, the adjective: "con-substantial" is a *technical* term which is used in *philosophy* and *theology* to define the *existential equality* of beings, signifying: "being of the same substance," "being of the same essence" or "being of the same nature," "having the same substance or essence or nature." Thus, we profess in our *Creed* that the Son of God is *con-substantial* with His Heavenly Father which means that the Son of God is absolutely of the same Divine nature with His Heavenly Father. This, in turn, entails their absolute *co-eternity* and *co-equality*; cf. D. P. Simpson, Cassell's Latin Dictionary (New York 1968), pp. 160.578; S. A. Handford – M. Herberg, Langenscheidt's Pocket Latin Dictionary (Berlin – Munich 1966), pp. 94.309; J. Morwood, The Pocket Oxford Latin Dictionary (Oxford 1995), p. 37; P. B. Gove, Webster's Third New International Dictionary of the English Language Unabridged (Springfield, Massachusetts 1993), p. 489.

to educate the People of God in accordance with what the Prophet Malachi says: "The lips of a priest should keep knowledge, and people should seek the Law from his mouth, for he is the messenger of the LORD of Hosts" (Malachi 2:7). The present book brings to light how many priests, called to be the messengers of the LORD of Hosts in order to lead the faithful entrusted to them according to the Law of God and of the Church, have lawlessly *mis*-led so many people, causing a huge disarray in the bosom of the Roman-Catholic Church throughout North America, because their priestly minds and hearts and lips did not keep knowledge.

This book consists of two main parts. The first part is devoted to the doctrine of the Catholic Church concerning the Most Blessed Sacrament of the Eucharist, whereas the second part deals with the profanation of the Eucharist. First I want to remind the reader of the very nature of the Eucharist and its very profound theological dimension, and then to turn his attention to the abuses of the Eucharist in the Church. By doing this, I want to reveal the gravity of the problem which I address, because the more one is aware of the Holiness of the Eucharist, the more he will be aware of the horror of the profanation of this Most Holy Sacrament, just as those who know about the biological processes that take place during a pregnancy see more clearly the crime of abortion. I hope that knowledge of the problem of criminal activity against our Eucharistic LORD, of which I write in this book, will deeply move the minds and hearts of those who are morally responsible for this most grievous sin; I hope that the message of this book will incline all of them to their total conversion.

PART I

An Epitome of the Teaching of the Catholic Church on the Most Holy Eucharist

Being fully aware that many Catholics today are neglected not only spiritually, but also intellectually and doctrinally, I intend, in this chapter, to delineate in a very condensed form the most principal, the most fundamental truths pertaining to the Sacrament of the Most Holy Communion, as they are being taught by the Magisterium of the Roman-Catholic Church over the centuries. And so, before I turn to the core of the problem, announced in the very title of the present book, let me first dwell on the theological mystery of the Sacrament of the Eucharist, because after more than twenty five years of my priestly service I have realized that more and more Catholics today are illiterate in their knowledge of the Roman-Catholic doctrine and in their faith. Theological knowledge nourishes faith, and faith completes the knowledge. In turn, the knowledge enlivened by faith increases awareness which stimulates a proper attitude and action. All the above is indispensable for being a mature follower of Jesus Christ.

1.

The Mystery of the Incarnation of God

*B*efore I advance to the very theme of the theological mystery of the Sacrament of the Eucharist, I wish first to comment on the profound mystery of the Divine Incarnation that has laid the foundation for the Sacrament of the Most Holy Body and Blood of our LORD Jesus Christ. In the article entitled: *Formula of Union*, the Ecumenical Council of Ephesus, held in 431, has expressed the mystery of the Incarnation of God with the following words:

> "We confess, then, our LORD Jesus Christ, the Only Begotten Son of God, perfect God and perfect Man of a rational Soul and a Body, begotten before all ages from the Father in His Godhead, the same in the last days, for us and for our salvation, born of Mary the Virgin, according to His humanity, one and the same consubstantial with the Father in Godhead and consubstantial with us in humanity, for a union of two natures took place. Therefore, we confess

one Christ, one Son, one LORD. According to this understanding of the unconfused union, we confess the Holy Virgin to be the Mother of God because God the Word took flesh and became Man and from His very conception united to Himself the temple He took from Her."[5]

This profound truth of our faith has been confirmed by the Ecumenical Council of Chalcedon which took place in 451. In their *Definition of the Faith*, the Fathers of the said council have professed:

"So, following the saintly Fathers, we all with one voice teach the confession of one and the same Son, our LORD Jesus Christ: the same perfect in Divinity and perfect in humanity, the same truly God and truly Man, of a rational Soul and a Body; consubstantial with the Father as regards His Divinity, and the same consubstantial with us as regards His humanity; like us in all respects except for sin (cf. Hebrews 4:15); begotten before the ages from the Father as regards His Divinity, and in the last days the same for us and for our salvation from Mary, the Virgin God-bearer, as regards His humanity; one and the same Christ, Son, LORD, Only Begotten, acknowledged in two natures which undergo no confusion, no change, no division, no separation; at no point was the difference between the natures taken away through the union, but rather the property of both natures is preserved and comes together

---

[5] N. P. Tanner, *vol. I*, op. cit., pp. 69–70.

into a single Person and a single subsistent Being; He is not parted or divided into two persons, but is one and the same Only Begotten Son, God, Word, LORD Jesus Christ, just as the Prophets taught from the beginning about Him, and as the LORD Jesus Christ Himself instructed us, and as the Creed of the Fathers handed it down to us."[6]

Following the Council of Ephesus and the Council of Chalcedon, the Second Ecumenical Council of Constantinople, held in 553, has stated:

"So, there is only one Christ, God and Man, the same being consubstantial with the Father in respect of His Divinity, and also consubstantial with us in respect of our humanity."[7]

And again, a very similar statement is found in the Third Ecumenical Council of Constantinople which was held in 680–681:

"[The council] professes our LORD Jesus Christ our true God, one of the Holy Trinity, [who] is of one same being and is the source of life, to be perfect in Divinity and perfect in humanity, the same truly God and truly Man, of a rational soul and a body; consubstantial with the Father as regards His Divinity, and the same consubstantial with us as regards His humanity; like us in all respects except for sin (cf. Hebrews 4:15); begotten before the ages from

---

[6] Ibid., pp. 86–87.
[7] Ibid., p. 118.

> the Father as regards His Divinity, and in the last days the same for us and for our salvation from the Holy Spirit and the Virgin Mary, who is properly and truly called Mother of God, as regards His humanity."[8]

Through the Act of Incarnation, the Son of God – who is eternally consubstantial with the Heavenly Father in His Divinity – has become consubstantial with us in His humanity. In this way, He has entered into our realm of existence which is the reality of time and space. This truth of our faith has been expressed by the Apostle Paul in one of his Christological hymns in which he writes that our LORD, "though He was in the form of God, He did not deem equality with God something to be grasped at. But He emptied Himself and took the form of a slave, being born in the likeness of men. He was known to be of human estate, and it was thus that He humbled Himself, obediently accepting even death, death on a cross" (Philippians 2:6–8; cf. Galatians 4:4–7).

But before His passion, when the Incarnate Son of God was about to depart from this world, in order to remain with us perpetually until the end of times, He has instituted the Sacrament of His Most Holy Body and Blood as His Living and Life-giving presence in the Church based on His consubstantiality with the Heavenly Father in His Divinity and on His consubstantiality with us in His humanity. This double consubstantiality, Divine and human, present in the Eucharist, expresses a perfect union of the Son of God with His Heavenly Father and simultaneously a perfect union of the Incarnate Son of God with us. This truth is to make us ever aware of the profundity of the Sacrament of the Most Holy Communion in which

---

[8] Ibid., p. 127.

our LORD Jesus Christ comes to us from the Heavenly Father, and through which we come to the Heavenly Father *through*, *with* and *in* His Only Begotten Incarnate Son. As God came to us by sharing in our humanity, so we come to God by sharing in His Divinity, according to what Saint Peter, the Apostle, writes in his Second Letter, namely, that we are "partakers of the Divine Nature" (2 Peter 1:4). First, the Son of God assumed our human nature, when He descended from heaven into the Immaculate Womb of the Blessed Virgin Mary who, giving Him humanity, bore true God and true Man, and then, the Incarnate Son of God has chosen bread and wine for the Eucharist in which He sustains His presence among us in time and space. As in the past, "the Word became flesh and dwelt among us" (John 1:14a) *historically*, so now, the Incarnate Word of God dwells among us *sacramentally*. Hence, the Eucharist is the *sacramental* prolongation and extension of the Incarnation of God in time and space, respectively.

2.

The Presence of Jesus Christ in Every Part of the Eucharist

The Ecumenical Council of Ephesus teaches on the Sacrament of the Eucharist, quoting the third letter of Saint Cyril of Alexandria to Nestorius[9] as follows:

> "Proclaiming the death according to the flesh of the Only Begotten Son of God, that is, Jesus Christ, and professing His return to life from the dead and His ascension into heaven, we offer the unbloody worship in the churches and so proceed to the mystical thanksgivings and are sanctified, having partaken of the Holy Flesh and Precious Blood of

---

[9] Nestorius (died ca. 451) was a native of Germanicia in Syria Euphratensis. He entered a monastery at Antioch where he was influenced by the Antiochene theological school. Soon he acquired a great reputation as a preacher. In 428, he became Archbishop of Constantinople. Nestorius rejected the title of *Theotokos*, the "God-bearer," for the Blessed Virgin Mary. Therefore, he was condemned and excommunicated at the Ecumenical Council of Ephesus on June 22, 431; cf. F. L. Cross – E. A. Livingstone, The Oxford Dictionary of the Christian Church (Oxford 1993), pp. 961–962.1365.

Christ, the Saviour of us all. This we receive not as ordinary flesh, heaven forbid, nor as that of a man who has been made holy and joined to the Word by union of honour, or who had a divine indwelling, but as truly the Life-giving and real Flesh of the Word. For being Life by nature as God, when He became one with His own Flesh, He made it also to be Life-giving, as also He said to us: 'Amen I say to you, unless you eat the Flesh of the Son of Man and drink His Blood' (John 6:53). For we must not think that it is the flesh of a man like us (for how can the flesh of man be life-giving by its own nature?), but as being made the true Flesh of the One who for our sake became the Son of Man and was called so."[10]

The Ecumenical Council of Trent, in Chapter 4 of the *Decree on the Most Holy Sacrament of the Eucharist*, entitled: *On transubstantiation*, formulated at its Session 13, held on October 11, 1551, has declared:

"... By the consecration of the bread and wine, there takes place the change of the whole substance of the bread into the substance of the Body of Christ our LORD, and of the whole substance of the wine into the substance of His Blood. And the Holy Catholic Church has suitably and properly called this change transubstantiation."[11]

---

[10] N. P. Tanner, *vol. I*, op. cit., pp. 54–55.
[11] Ibid., *vol. II*, op. cit., p. 695.

This dogmatic statement of the Fathers of the Council of Trent renders the most fundamental truth concerning the very nature of the Eucharist, namely, that by the Divine power of the Words of Consecration, the whole substance of the bread and the whole substance of the wine are changed into the substance of the Body and Blood of our LORD Jesus Christ. Here, the word: "whole" is fundamental. Using the expression: "the whole substance of the bread and the whole substance of the wine," which are changed into the substance of the Body and Blood of Christ, the Church wants to enhance the fact that after the consecration nothing, absolutely nothing, remains from the substance of the bread and from the substance of the wine, but the whole substance of the bread and the whole substance of the wine are changed into the substance of the Body and Blood of Christ. In this manner, the Church instructs the faithful that the Consecrated Bread and the Consecrated Wine, visible to our senses, are by no means to be understood as a kind of "vessels" which contain the substance of the Body and Blood of Christ, since the Consecrated Bread and the Consecrated Wine *ARE* the *VERY SUBSTANCE* of the Body and Blood of our LORD Jesus Christ.

Now, how can we explain this extraordinary and unique mystery of our faith. Here, Aristotle (384–322 B.C.), the greatest philosopher of ancient Greece, comes to our aid. In his metaphysics, Aristotle taught that material creatures possess their substance and accidents, that is, appearances.[12] The substance is invisible for the human senses as opposed to the accidents which are visible. To expound this issue, let me use a very simple example. For instance, someone has a white shirt. The shirt has its substance and its accident which is a white color; however, this same shirt can be dyed black. What would be the result? The substance of the shirt would remain 100%

---

[12] Cf. F. L. Cross – E. A. Livingstone, op. cit., pp. 85.1390.

the same, because this would be the same shirt, only the accident would change, that is, the color. The shirt which looked white before would look black. The shirt would have exactly the same substance, but it would look different only in appearance.

Now, as regards the consecration of the bread and wine, something diametrically opposite takes place, namely, the accidents of the bread and wine, which are perceptible by the senses, that is to say, their color and their taste remain the same, but their whole substance, which is not perceptible by the senses, is totally changed into the substance of the Body and Blood of Christ.[13] Therefore, *after* the Words of Consecration, the Consecrated Bread and the Consecrated Wine still look as bread and wine, and they taste as bread and wine; however, their whole substance is no longer the substance of bread and wine, but the substance of the Living and Life-giving Body and Blood of Christ.

The Ecumenical Council of Trent, in Chapter 1 of the above-mentioned *Decree on the Most Holy Sacrament of the Eucharist*, entitled: *On the real presence of our LORD Jesus Christ in the Most Holy Sacrament of the Eucharist*, states the following:

> "In the first place, the holy council teaches and openly and without qualification professes that, after the consecration of the bread and the wine, our LORD Jesus Christ, true God and true Man, is *truly, really and substantially* (vere, realiter ac substantialiter) contained in the propitious Sacrament of the Holy Eucharist under the appearance of those things which are perceptible to the senses.

---

[13] Cf. ibid., pp. 9–10.

Nor are the two assertions incompatible, that our Saviour is ever seated in Heaven at the right hand of the Father in His natural mode of existing, and that He is nevertheless sacramentally present to us by His substance in many other places in a mode of existing which, though we can hardly express it in words, we can grasp with minds enlightened by faith as possible to God (cf. Matthew 19:26; Luke 18:27) and must most firmly believe. For thus did all our forefathers, as many as were in the true Church of Christ and treated of this Most Holy Sacrament, most clearly profess: namely, that our Redeemer at the Last Supper instituted this so admirable sacrament when He bore witness in express and unambiguous words that, after the blessing of the bread and the wine, He was offering to them His own Body and His own Blood. Since those words, recorded by the Holy Evangelists (cf. Matthew 26:26–28; Mark 14:22–24; Luke 22:19–20) and afterwards repeated by Saint Paul (cf. 1 Corinthians 11:24–25), bear that proper and very clear meaning which the fathers understood them to have, it is surely a most intolerable and shameful deed for some base and argumentative persons to twist them to false and imaginary meanings that deny the reality of Christ's Flesh and Blood, against the universal understanding of the Church which, as *the pillar and bulwark of the Truth* (1 Timothy 3:15), detests these contrived theories of evil people as the work of the devil, and constantly recalls and confesses with gratitude this outstanding favour of Christ."[14]

All seven sacraments are holy, and are the Divine instruments of our Salvation, for in all of them, our LORD Jesus Christ is present with *His Divine* and *saving power*; however, *ONLY* in the Sacrament of the Most Holy Communion is He present with *His Divine Nature*. It is the Eucharist and *exclusively* the Eucharist that makes the *very Substance of the Divine Nature of our LORD* present in the Church, and not only in the Church, but in the whole universe as well. God, who is above the entire created world, lives in the world *through* and *in* the Most Holy Eucharist. It is *ONLY* in this Blessed Sacrament that we are able to touch the *very Nature of His Divinity* in a *sacramental* manner (cf. 2 Peter 1:4; 1 John 1:1).

The exclusiveness and the superiority of the Sacrament of the Most Holy Communion to the other sacraments have been confirmed by the above-mentioned Ecumenical Council of Trent. In Chapter 3 of the above-quoted *Decree on the Most Holy Sacrament of the Eucharist*, entitled: *On the excellence of the Most Holy Eucharist over the other sacraments*, the said council teaches:

> "There is indeed this which is common to the Most Holy Eucharist along with the other sacraments: it is a sign of sacred reality and the visible form of invisible grace. But in it there is found the excelling and unique quality that, whereas the other sacraments first have the force of sanctifying at the moment when one uses them, in the Eucharist

---

[14] N. P. Tanner, *vol. II*, op. cit., pp. 693–694.

the Author of Holiness Himself is present before their use. For the Apostles had not yet received the Eucharist from the hand of the LORD (cf. Matthew 26:26; Mark 14:22; Luke 22:19) when He declared with all Truth that it was His own Body which He was offering. And it has at all times been the belief in the Church of God that immediately after the consecration the true Body of our LORD and His true Blood exist along with His Soul and Divinity under the form of bread and wine. The Body is present under the form of bread and the Blood under the form of wine, by virtue of the Words. The same Body, however, is under the form of wine and the Blood under the form of bread, and the Soul under either form, by virtue of that natural link and concomitance by which the parts of Christ the LORD, who has now risen from the dead and will die no more (cf. Romans 6:9), are mutually united. The Divinity, too, is present by that marvellous hypostatic union with His Body and Soul. Hence it is entirely true that as much is contained under one of the forms as under both; for Christ exists whole and entire under the form of bread and under any part of that form, and likewise whole under the form of wine and under its parts."[15]

In the above-adduced text of the Council of Trent, one sentence is extremely significant that as regards the Eucharistic Body and Blood of Christ "the same Body [...] is under the form of wine and the Blood under

---

[15] Ibid., pp. 694–695.

the form of bread." By this statement, the Church wants to teach us the profound Mystery of the Most Holy Eucharist that the Consecrated Bread is not only the Body of Christ, neither is the Consecrated Wine only the Blood of Christ, because then the Consecrated Bread would not make present the whole and entire Jesus Christ, neither would the Consecrated Wine make present the whole and entire Jesus Christ, but as it truly is, the Body of Christ is present both under the form of the Consecrated Bread and under the form of the Consecrated Wine, as well as the Blood of Christ is present both under the form of the Consecrated Wine and under the form of the Consecrated Bread. Therefore, when a priest distributes the Eucharist and gives to a person the Consecrated Bread, saying: "the Body of Christ," it does not mean at all that the person receives only the Body of Christ, and when a priest gives to a person the Consecrated Wine, saying: "the Blood of Christ," it does not mean at all that the person receives only the Blood of Christ. Teaching that Jesus Christ exists in the Eucharist whole and entire as much under one of the forms as under both, as well as under any part of the Eucharistic species, be it the parts of the Consecrated Bread and/ or the parts of the Consecrated Wine, the Ecumenical Council of Trent emphatically stresses that the Consecrated Bread and/ or the Consecrated Wine, as well as any part of the Consecrated Bread and/ or any part of the Consecrated Wine, form one and undivided reality of the presence of the whole and entire Jesus Christ. However, speaking still more precisely, one must say that Jesus Christ is not only undivided, but He is even indivisible in the Eucharist. In a word, it is impossible to divide our LORD in the Eucharist, and/ or to receive Him only partially. It doesn't matter whether or not someone receives the Eucharist under one or two species, because absolutely the whole and entire Jesus Christ is present in every part, even the smallest part, of the Eucharist with His Divinity and Humanity, Body, Blood and Soul. What is, then, the difference between those who receive the Most Holy Communion under one kind and those who receive it under both kinds? The answer is one and the only one: the difference is absolutely ZERO! Therefore, a person who receives the Eucharist under one form does not receive anything less than a person who receives it under both forms, and a person who receives the Eucharist under both forms does not receive anything more than a person who receives it under one form. Because, as the above-quoted Council of Trent rightly teaches: "It is entirely true that as much is contained under one of the forms as under both; for Christ exists whole and entire under the form of bread and under any part of that form, and likewise whole under the form of wine and under its parts."[16]

The Ecumenical Council of Trent, in its *Canons on the Most Holy Sacrament of the Eucharist*, formulated at Session 13, held on October 11, 1551, states in Canon 1:

> "If anyone denies that in the Most Holy Sacrament of the Eucharist there are contained *truly, really and substantially* (vere, realiter et substantialiter), the Body and Blood of our LORD Jesus Christ together with the Soul and Divinity, and therefore the whole Christ, but says that He is present in it only as in a sign or figure or by His power: let him be anathema."[17]

---

[16] Ibid., p. 695.
[17] Ibid., p. 697.

And in Canon 3, the Fathers of the said Council of Trent continue, admonishing the faithful:

> "If anyone denies that the whole Christ is contained in the venerable Sacrament of the Eucharist under each form, and under each part of each form when it is divided: let him be anathema."[18]

Thus, the above-quoted ecclesiastical documents unequivocally affirm that there is no *essential* difference in receiving the Most Holy Communion under one or under both forms, inasmuch as every particle of this Most Blessed Sacrament is the real presence of the Eucharistic Jesus Christ our LORD who gives Himself to the recipients – *totally*.

---

[18] Ibid.

3.

The Eucharist under the Form of the Consecrated Bread Alone

Now, I wish to make a short comment on the issue of why receiving the Eucharist under both species, that is, under the forms of Consecrated Bread and Wine is absolutely unnecessary. Let me first adduce a text taken from the legacy of the Ecumenical Council of Constance held in 1414–1418. On June 15, 1415, at Session 13, the Fathers of the aforementioned council accepted, authorized and promulgated the document of the following contents:

> "In the Name of the Holy and undivided Trinity, Father and Son and Holy Spirit, Amen. Certain people, in some parts of the world, have rashly dared to assert that the Christian people ought to receive the Holy Sacrament of the Eucharist under the forms of both bread and wine. They communicate the laity everywhere not only under the form of bread, but also under that of wine, and they

stubbornly assert that they should communicate even after a meal, or else without the need of a fast, contrary to the Church's custom which has been laudably and sensibly approved, from the Church's head downwards, but which they damnably try to repudiate as sacrilegious. Therefore, this present General Council of Constance, legitimately assembled in the Holy Spirit, wishing to provide for the safety of the faithful against this error, after long deliberation by many persons learned in Divine and human law, declares, decrees and defines that, although Christ instituted this venerable sacrament after a meal and ministered it to His Apostles under the forms of both bread and wine (cf. Matthew 26:26–28; Mark 14:22–24; Luke 22:19–20; 1 Corinthians 11:23–27), nevertheless and notwithstanding this, the praiseworthy authority of the sacred canons and the approved custom of the Church have and do retain that this sacrament ought not to be celebrated after a meal nor received by the faithful without fasting, except in cases of sickness or some other necessity as permitted by law or by the Church. Moreover, just as this custom was sensibly introduced in order to avoid various dangers and scandals, so with similar or even greater reason was it possible to introduce and sensibly observe the custom that, although this sacrament was received by the faithful under both kinds in the Early Church, nevertheless later it was received under both kinds only by those confecting it, and by the laity only under the form of bread. For it should be very firmly believed, and in no way doubted, that the *whole Body* and *Blood of Christ* are truly contained under both the form of bread and the form of wine. Therefore, since this custom was introduced for good reasons by the Church and holy Fathers, and has been observed for a very long time, it should be held as a law which nobody may repudiate or alter at will without the Church's permission. To say that the observance of this custom or law is sacrilegious or illicit must be regarded as erroneous. Those who stubbornly assert the opposite of the aforesaid are to be confined as heretics and severely punished by the local bishops or their officials or the [executives] of heresy in the kingdoms or provinces in which anything is attempted or presumed against this decree, according to the canonical and legitimate sanctions that have been wisely established in favour of the Catholic faith against heretics and their supporters.

This holy synod also decrees and declares, regarding this matter, that instructions are to be sent to the most reverend fathers and lords in Christ, patriarchs, primates, archbishops, bishops, and their vicars in spirituals, wherever they may be, in which they are to be commissioned and ordered on the authority of this sacred council and under pain of excommunication, to punish effectively those who err against this decree. They may receive back into the Church's fold those who have gone astray by communicating the people under the forms of both bread and wine, and have taught this, provided they repent and after a salutary penance, in accordance with the measure of their fault, has been enjoined upon them. They are to repress as heretics, however, by means of the Church's censures and even if necessary by calling in the help of the secular arm, those of them whose hearts have become hardened and who are unwilling to return to penance."[19]

The most important statement expressed in the above-quoted text is that "the *whole Body* and *Blood of Christ* are truly contained under both the form of bread and the form of wine." This truth was later confirmed by the Ecumenical Council of Florence at Session 8, held on November 22, 1439, during which the Catholic Church once again reminded all the faithful of the profound Mystery of the Blessed Sacrament of the Eucharist in the following words:

"The form of this sacrament are the words of the Saviour with which He effected this sacrament. A priest speaking in the person of Christ effects this sacrament. For, in virtue of those words, the substance of bread is changed into the Body of Christ and the substance of wine into His Blood. In such wise, however, that the *whole Christ* is contained both under the form of bread and under the form of wine; under any part of the Consecrated Host as

---

[19] Ibid., *vol. I*, op. cit., pp. 418–419.

well as after division of the Consecrated Wine, there is the *whole Christ*."[20]

Therefore, the receiving of the Sacrament of the Most Holy Communion under both species is absolutely unnecessary, since the *whole Christ* is present under the form of the Consecrated Bread and/ or under the form of the Consecrated Wine.

The Ecumenical Council of Trent has also broached the issue of whether or not the Eucharist should be received by laity and non-consecrating clergy under both forms. The said council, at its Session 21, held on July 16, 1562, in its document *Teaching on Communion under both kinds and of children*, in Chapter 1, entitled: *Laity and non-consecrating clergy are not bound by Divine command to Communion under both kinds*, declares the following:

> "... Laity and clergy who are not consecrating are under no Divine command to receive the Sacrament of the Eucharist under both kinds; and |...| it can in no way be doubted (with integrity in faith) that Communion under either kind is sufficient for their salvation. For, though Christ the LORD instituted this revered sacrament at the Last Supper and gave it to the Apostles in the forms of bread and wine, this institution and gift do not mean that all the faithful are bound by a precept of the LORD to receive both forms. Nor is it correct to deduce from that saying in the sixth chapter of John that Communion in both kinds was commanded by the LORD, however it may be understood from

---

[20] Ibid., pp. 546–547.

different interpretations of the holy fathers and doctors. For He who said, 'unless you eat the Flesh of the Son of Man and drink His Blood, you have no life in you' (John 6:53b), also said, 'if anyone eats of this bread, he will live for ever' (John 6:51b). And He who said, 'he who eats My Flesh and drinks My Blood has Eternal Life' (John 6:54), also said, 'the bread which I shall give for the life of the world is My Flesh' (John 6:51c). And finally, He who said, 'he who eats My Flesh and drinks My Blood abides in Me, and I in him' (John 6:56), said as well, 'he who eats this bread will live for ever' (John 6:58b)."[21]

In the same document *Teaching on Communion under both kinds and of children*, in Chapter 2, entitled: *The power of the Church in administering the Sacrament of the Eucharist*, the Fathers of the aforementioned council write as follows:

"The council further declares that the Church always had the power in administering the sacraments of making dispositions and changes it judged expedient for the well-being of recipients, or for the reverence due to the sacraments themselves, provided their essentials remained intact, in view of changing affairs, times and places. This the Apostle seems to have indicated plainly enough when he said: 'This is how one should regard us, as servants of Christ and stewards of the mysteries of God' (1 Corinthians 4:1);

---

[21] Ibid., *vol. II*, p. 726.

and it is surely clear that he himself used this power, not only in many other matters, but over this sacrament too, when after giving some instructions for its conduct he said: 'About the other things I will give directions when I come' (1 Corinthians 11:34b). Although from the beginning of Christian worship the use of both kinds was common, yet that custom was very widely changed in the course of time; and so Holy Mother Church, acknowledging her authority over the administration of the sacraments and influenced by good and serious reasons, has approved this custom of communicating in one form and has decreed this to be its rule, which is not to be condemned nor freely changed without the Church's own authority."[22]

What is conspicuous in the declarations of the Fathers of both the Council of Constance and the Council of Trent is the fact that it was for good and serious reasons that the Catholic Church introduced the custom of distributing the Eucharist under the form of the Consecrated Bread alone for lay people and clergy who are not consecrating in order to avoid various dangers and scandals. The Fathers of the Council of Constance and of the Council of Trent do not clarify explicitly the reasons for which the distribution of the Most Holy Communion under the form of the Consecrated Bread alone was introduced, but two main reasons seem to be in mind of the Fathers of the aforementioned councils: (1) a protection of the Consecrated Wine from being accidentally spilled out; (2) a dangerous and scandalous profanation of the Most Holy Blood of Christ by careless ministers. One

---

[22] Ibid., pp. 726–727.

thing is absolutely sure and beyond any doubt that the reasons had to be extremely serious, because the Fathers of the Council of Constance determined that no priest might communicate the people under the forms of both the Consecrated Bread and the Consecrated Wine "under pain of excommunication."[23] Such a restriction is reserved in the Church only for matters of the greatest importance. Therefore, one can surmise that these good and serious reasons, by which the Church was influenced, may refer to the abuses of the Most Blessed Sacrament of the Eucharist which, in the past, took place in the Church.

As it unequivocally follows from the above-quoted texts of the Council of Constance and of the Council of Trent, the receiving of the Eucharist under the form of the *Consecrated Bread alone* is theologically correct and absolutely sufficient for one's salvation, because the Eucharistic Jesus is indivisible, being wholly present in any part of the Eucharist. Consequently, the Council of Trent declares in the above-adduced document *Teaching on Communion under both kinds and of children*, in Chapter 3, entitled: *Christ is received whole and entire under either kind, as is the true sacrament*, the following:

> "... Although our Redeemer instituted this sacrament at the Last Supper and gave it to the Apostles in two forms, as was said above; it must nevertheless be asserted that Christ is also received whole and entire, as is the true sacrament, under either kind alone, and that therefore, as far as the

---

[23] Ibid., *vol. I*, p. 419.

effect is concerned, those who receive only one form are not cheated of any grace necessary for salvation."[24]

Therefore, the same Council of Trent, in its *Canons on Communion under both kinds and of children*, in Canon 3, strongly enacts the following:

> "If anyone says that Christ, the Source and Author of all Graces, is not received *whole* and *entire* under the one form of bread, on the grounds that He is not then received under both forms according to Christ's institution, as some would falsely assert: let him be anathema."[25]

The above-quoted texts reveal a great solicitude of the Catholic Church, in the past, for the Most Blessed Sacrament of the Eucharist. By a very austere disciplinary restriction, imposed by the Ecclesiastical Authorities with regard to the distribution of Holy Communion under the form of the *Consecrated Bread alone* for the laity and the non-consecrating clergy, the Church significantly reduced the opportunities for the profanation of the Eucharist. In this way, the Church protected the faithful from this most grievous sin.

---

[24] Ibid., *vol. II*, op. cit., p. 727; see also p. 695.
[25] Ibid., p. 727.

4.

The Salvific and Sanctifying Power of the Eucharist

The Council of Trent continued the theme of the Eucharist at its Session 22, held on September 17, 1562, and in Chapter 2 of its document, entitled: *Teaching and canons on the Most Holy Sacrifice of the Mass*, the Fathers of the said council have written about the Eucharist as follows:

> "In this Divine Sacrifice which is performed in the Mass, the *very same* Christ is contained and offered in Bloodless manner who made a bloody Sacrifice of Himself once for all on the Cross. Hence the holy council teaches that this is a truly propitiatory Sacrifice, and brings it about that if we approach God with sincere hearts and upright faith, and with awe and reverence, 'we receive mercy and find grace to help in time of need' (Hebrews 4:16). For the LORD is appeased by this Offering, He gives the gracious

gift of repentance, He absolves even enormous offences and sins. For it is one and the same Victim here offering Himself by the ministry of His priests, who then offered Himself on the Cross: it is only the manner of offering that is different. For the benefits of that Sacrifice (namely the Sacrifice of Blood) are received in the fullest measure through the Bloodless Offering, so far is this latter in any way from impairing the value of the former. Therefore, it is quite properly offered according to Apostolic Tradition not only for the sins, penalties, satisfactions and other needs of the faithful who are living, but also for those who have died in Christ, but are not yet fully cleansed."[26]

And in Chapter 4 of the above-adduced document, the Council of Trent teaches on the Eucharist, saying:

> "Holy things must be treated in a holy way, *and this Sacrifice is the Holiest of all things* (sitque hoc omnium sanctissimum sacrificium)."[27]

Speaking about the Eucharist as the Sacrifice that is "the Holiest of all things," the Council of Trent indicates the superiority of the Blessed Sacrament of the true Body and Blood of our LORD to anything else in the Church. Using the superlative form: "holiest" in reference to the Eucharist, the Fathers of the said council remind the faithful that there is nothing in

---

[26] Ibid., pp. 733–734.
[27] Ibid., p. 734.

the spiritual life of the Church that surpasses this sacrament which is an absolutely Unique and Exquisite Gift from God; therefore, it must be cherished by the faithful with the most profound love and reverence.

The Second Vatican Council, at Session 3, held on December 4, 1963, in Paragraph 2 of its *Constitution on the Sacred Liturgy* "Sacrosanctum Concilium," teaches:

> "... The liturgy, through which, especially in the Divine Sacrifice of the Eucharist, 'the act of our redemption is being carried out (*Roman Missal*, prayer over the gifts for 9th Sunday after Pentecost),' becomes thereby the chief means through which believers are expressing in their lives and demonstrating to others the mystery which is Christ, and the sort of entity the true Church really is."[28]

This is a very profound and powerful catechesis of the Roman-Catholic Church: the Blessed Sacrament of the Eucharist makes our Redeemer present among us, because the Eucharist is – JESUS CHRIST HIMSELF. The entity of Christians comes from – CHRIST; therefore, the Eucharist is for us believers the chief, visible and tangible means through which our Christian entity is manifested in this world. Consequently, any act of profanation of the Most Holy Eucharist is an act against our Christian entity; such an act is a kind of spiritual suicide!

The said council, in the above-cited constitution, in Chapter 2, entitled: *The Holy Mystery which is the Eucharist*, states in Paragraph 47 the following:

---

[28] Ibid., p. 820.

> "Our Saviour inaugurated the Eucharist Sacrifice of His Body and Blood at the Last Supper on the night He was betrayed, in order to make His Sacrifice of the Cross last throughout time until He should return; and indeed to entrust a token to the Church, His beloved [spouse], by which to remember His Death and Resurrection."[29]

This teaching of the Church is based on the Scriptural data. The Apostle Paul writes in his First Letter to the faithful at Corinth in the following words: "For I received from the LORD that which I also delivered to you: that the LORD Jesus on the same night in which He was betrayed took bread; and when He had given thanks, He broke it and said, 'Take, eat; this is My Body which is broken for you; do this in remembrance of Me.' In the same manner, He also took the cup after supper, saying, 'This cup is the New Covenant in My Blood. This do, as often as you drink it, in remembrance of Me.' For as often as you eat this bread and drink this cup, you proclaim the LORD's death till He comes. Therefore, whoever eats this Bread or drinks this Cup of the LORD in an unworthy manner will be guilty of the Body and Blood of the LORD" (1 Corinthians 11:23–27). In these words, Saint Paul professes his faith and the faith of the Primeval Church in the real presence of Jesus Christ in the Eucharist. If the Eucharist were only a "symbol" of the Body and Blood of Christ, then no one who eats the Consecrated Bread or drinks the Consecrated Wine in an unworthy manner would be guilty of the Body and Blood of the LORD. This is so self-evident that it does not need any further comment.

---

[29] Ibid., p. 830.

The Second Vatican Council, at its Session 5, held on November 21, 1964, promulgated the *Dogmatic Constitution on the Church* "Lumen Gentium." In Chapter 1 of this constitution, which is entitled: *The Mystery of the Church*, in Paragraph 3, the Fathers of the said council write:

> "As often as the Sacrifice of the Cross, by which 'Christ, our Paschal Lamb, has been sacrificed' (1 Corinthians 5:7b), is celebrated on the altar, there is effected the work of our redemption. At the same time, through the Sacrament of the Eucharistic Bread, there is represented and produced the unity of the faithful, who make up one Body in Christ (cf. 1 Corinthians 10:17)."[30]

The Apostle Paul teaches that "because there is one bread, we who are many are one body, for we all partake of the one bread" (1 Corinthians 10:17). Thus, the Eucharist confirms, strengthens and rejuvenates the spiritual life and the existential union of every individual Christian and the entire Church with Jesus Christ, the union into which every Christian has entered through the Sacrament of Baptism. The Eucharist continuously vivifies the interior life of the Church, inasmuch as its very power comes from the real presence of our LORD Jesus Christ who is Living and Life-giving in this Most Blessed Sacrament. Therefore, Holy Communion is for us the Greatest Gift from Heaven, since it is *ONLY* in this sacrament that we touch the Divine Nature of our LORD already here, on earth (cf. 2 Peter 1:4; 1 John 1:1).

---

[30] Ibid., p. 850.

The significance of the Most Holy Eucharist, in the life of the faithful, is expressed, among other things, in different titles which the Catholic Church uses in reference to this Blessed Sacrament. The Ecumenical Council of Constance calls the Eucharist: "Venerable Sacrament,"[31] and the Fathers of the Council of Trent name the Eucharist: "Admirable Sacrament,"[32] "Sublime and Venerable Sacrament,"[33] "Revered Sacrament,"[34] "Wondrous Sacrament,"[35] "True and Unique Sacrifice,"[36] "the Propitious Sacrament,"[37] "Truly Propitiatory Sacrifice," "Divine Sacrifice,"[38] "Heavenly Sacrament," "Sacred Quality and Divinity,"[39] "the Most Awesome and Holy Sacrament,"[40] "Awesome Mystery,"[41] "the Most Holy Sacrifice,"[42] "the Holiest of all things (omnium sanctissimum)."[43]

Likewise, the Fathers of the Second Vatican Council apply their profound expressions to the Sacrament of the Most Holy Communion, calling it: "the Holy Mystery," "the Immaculate Victim,"[44] "the Sacrifice of the Cross,"[45] "the Divine Sacrifice of the Eucharist,"[46] "the Eucharistic

---

[31] Ibid., *vol. I*, p. 419.
[32] Ibid., *vol. II*, p. 694.
[33] Ibid., p. 695; see also p. 697.
[34] Ibid., pp. 726.701.
[35] Ibid., p. 697.
[36] Ibid., p. 732.
[37] Ibid., p. 693.
[38] Ibid., p. 733.
[39] Ibid., p. 696.
[40] Ibid., pp. 726.694.
[41] Ibid., p. 736.
[42] Ibid., p. 737.
[43] Ibid., p. 734.
[44] Ibid., p. 830.
[45] Ibid., pp. 830.850.
[46] Ibid., p. 820.

Sacrifice, the Source and the Culmination of all Christian life,"[47] "[the] Most Noble Sacrament,"[48] "a sacrament of faithful relationships, a sign of unity, a bond of Divine Love, a special Easter Meal."[49]

The Roman-Catholic Church teaches in Canon 897 of the *Code of Canon Law*: "The Most Holy Eucharist is the Most August Sacrament, in which Christ the LORD Himself is contained, offered and received, and by which the Church constantly lives and grows. The Eucharistic Sacrifice, the Memorial of the Death and Resurrection of the LORD, in which the Sacrifice of the Cross is perpetuated over the centuries, is the summit and the source of all Christian worship and life; it signifies and effects the unity of the People of God and achieves the building up of the Body of Christ. The other sacraments and all the ecclesiastical works of the apostolate are closely related to the Holy Eucharist and are directed to it."[50] Again, we read in Canon 898 of the *Code of Canon Law*: "The faithful are to hold the Eucharist in highest honor, taking part in the Celebration of the Most August Sacrifice, receiving the sacrament devoutly and frequently, and worshiping it with supreme adoration; pastors, clarifying the doctrine on this sacrament, are to instruct the faithful thoroughly about this obligation."[51] The Eucharistic Liturgy is – as the Second Vatican Council states in its *Constitution on the Sacred Liturgy* from Session 3 held on December 4, 1963 – "the high point towards which the activity of the Church is directed and, simultaneously, the source from which all its power flows out."[52] The

---

[47] Ibid., p. 857.
[48] Ibid.
[49] Ibid., p. 830.
[50] *Code of Canon Law. Latin–English Edition. Translation prepared under the auspices of the Canon Law Society of America* (Washington, D.C. 1983), p. 337.
[51] Ibid.
[52] N. P. Tanner, *vol. II*, op. cit., p. 823.

Fathers of the said council teach in the same *Constitution on the Sacred Liturgy* that the liturgy, especially the Divine Sacrifice of the Eucharist, "is each day building up those who are within into a holy temple in the LORD, into a dwelling place for God in the Spirit (cf. Ephesians 2:21–22)."[53] "No other activity of the Church equals it in terms of its official recognition or its degree of effectiveness."[54] As it follows from the above-quoted ecclesiastical texts, the Most Blessed Sacrament of the Body and Blood of our LORD Jesus Christ is the very center and the very heart of the spiritual life of the Church. Therefore, the Most Holy Eucharist is absolutely vital for all Christians, not only for Catholics. Saint Ignatius of Antioch describes the Eucharistic Blood of Christ as "Love that cannot perish."[55] All these aforenamed titles and expressions concerning the Eucharist unequivocally prove how profoundly the Mother Church treasures and cherishes this absolutely unique and exquisite sacrament.

At the time of the Old Testament, the Holy of Holies was the place – in the Meeting Tent and later in the Jerusalem Temple – into which the high priest was privileged to enter and only once a year, that is, on the Day of Atonement, where he was able to reach the climax of his encounter with God YHWH on earth (cf. Leviticus 16:1–19; Numbers 29:7–11). There was no other place – not only on earth, but also in the entire universe – which would be holier than the Holy of Holies; nevertheless, God was present in this exclusive place only with His Divine power, not with His Divine Nature. Today, at the time of the New Testament, the Most Holy Eucharist replaces the Old Testament Holy of Holies, but, as opposed to the Holy of

---

[53] Ibid., p. 820.

[54] Ibid., p. 822.

[55] "From a letter to the Romans by Saint Ignatius, bishop and martyr," [in]: *The Liturgy of the Hours, vol. IV* (New York 1975), p. 1491.

Holies, our LORD is present not only with His Divine power, but with His Divine Nature, as well. The Eucharist is the very presence of our LORD Jesus Christ not only in the Church, not only on the entire earth, but in the whole universe. Indeed, the Most Holy Communion is:

- the New Testament Holy of Holies;
- the Most Contemplative Sacrament;
- the Sacrament of the Eucharistic Incarnate Word of God.

In this Most Blessed Sacrament, our LORD Jesus Christ, the Incarnate Word of God in Eucharistic form, speaks to us with His sanctifying, permeating and piercing silence (cf. Hebrews 4:12). Therefore, the above-mentioned Fathers of the Council of Trent rightly teach that the Most Holy Eucharist is "the Holiest of all things (omnium sanctissimum)."[56] This means that nothing in the Church, nothing on earth, nothing in the entire universe and the whole universe as such can *qualitatively* match even the tiniest crumb of the Consecrated Bread and/ or the tiniest drop of the Consecrated Wine, inasmuch as every, even the most microscopic, particle of the Most Holy Eucharist is vibrant with the absolute and limitless, infinite and inconceivable Divine Life. In our present world, the Eucharist is the only possible reality in which the Divine substance descends to man, and in which man touches the Divine substance already here, on earth. Accordingly, this unique and exquisite sacrament must be honored with utmost respect by all of us Christians who form together with our LORD one Mystical Body (cf. Romans 12:4–5; 1 Corinthians 6:15a; 10:17; Ephesians 1:10.22–23; Colossians 1:18), and if it is so, then also

---

[56] N. P. Tanner, *vol. II*, op. cit., p. 734.

with the Most Holy Eucharist, because it is impossible to separate Jesus Christ from the Eucharist; *JESUS CHRIST AND THE EUCHARIST ARE ABSOLUTELY ONE!* Therefore, we must also be mindful of this august, venerable, revered Mystery of our Faith, and remember that the way we treat the Eucharist is the way we treat Jesus Christ Himself. When I see how routinely some people receive the Eucharist, I ask myself whether or not they are really aware of *WHOM* they receive.

At this point, I want to remind all Catholics that those who do not believe in the real presence of Jesus Christ in the Most Holy Communion must not receive this sacrament. The Eucharist is NOT a kind of "magic," but the very Body and Blood of our LORD Jesus Christ, the Incarnate Son of the Living God, who is to be welcomed to our hearts with ardent love and living faith, and not merely by a physical gesture, inasmuch as the Eucharist received without faith has no spiritual impact on the receiver. It is not only the Sacrament of Baptism and being in the state of God's Grace which give us access to Holy Communion, but also our faith. This is a very serious issue, because a lack of faith in the real presence of Jesus Christ in the Eucharist has led in the past and even today leads many, very many Catholics, both from among the clergy and the laity, to the profanation of this so Precious and Holy a Sacrament.

Before closing this chapter, two absolutely fundamental theological and liturgical truths must be stressed very emphatically: (1) the Catholic Church firmly teaches that whenever the Eucharist is celebrated, the Sacrifice of our LORD is really at work within the Church; (2) during the Holy Mass, the Sacrifice of the Cross is NOT repeated, but only *made present* in our time and in our space. Whenever the Eucharist is celebrated, the *same* Jesus Christ is present as He was present among those who lived at the time, when He was present *historically* on earth, with only one difference, namely, that now He is present *sacramentally*, but still with His real Divinity and humanity. The Eucharist is the perpetuation of the real presence of our LORD Jesus Christ in the Church, the presence which is absolutely Holy; therefore, it must be cherished by us with the most profound holiness. Having in mind all these theological truths about the Divine Nature and the Mystery of the Most Holy Eucharist, we move now to the next chapter which deals with the abusive liturgical practices, in the bosom of the Roman-Catholic Church, through which this Most Blessed Sacrament is being desecrated.

PART II

The Profanation of the Sacrament of the Most Holy Eucharist in the Roman-Catholic Church

The second part of this book consists of three chapters: in the first chapter, there are presented the liturgical abuses of the Most Holy Eucharist by some irresponsible Catholics; in the second chapter, a message is sent to all those priests who profane the Most Precious Blood of Jesus Christ, calling them to a total conversion; in the third chapter, a fervent appeal is addressed to all Catholics, calling them to a profound respect for the Most Holy Sacrament of the True Body and Blood of our LORD, as well as encouraging them to take action.

1.

Sacrilegious Practices of the Profanation of the Eucharist

*I*n this chapter, I want to broach the problem of the liturgical abuses of the Sacrament of Holy Communion. Some of the cases I witnessed personally and some others I learned from faithful priests and pious lay people who shared their stories with me regarding the desecration of this Most Blessed Sacrament.

My first bad experience, as a priest, pertaining to a lack of respect for the Eucharist goes back to the Fall of 1991. During Advent of that year, I was invited, on a Sunday evening, to a parish to hear confessions. I came to the sacristy of the church where several priests were already gathered together before the penitential liturgy. While I was waiting there for the service, I observed on a table two chalices filled, as I believed, with wine. Thinking that they were prepared for the evening Mass, I asked the associate pastor, who had invited me to hear confessions, whether he would be celebrating an evening Mass, but he responded that there was no evening Mass in his parish on Sundays. When I asked him what the above-mentioned chalices, filled with wine, were for, he told me that they contained the Consecrated Wine that was not consumed during the previous Masses, and that he would later bring the chalices to the tabernacle. My heart almost stopped beating, when I realized how the Blood of Christ had been left completely unprotected. I was the only one who paid close attention to these abandoned chalices with the Blood of Christ. The other priests stood chatting and were completely unaware of what the chalices were holding. Practically any one of us could accidentally have touched the chalices and spilled the Blood of Christ. Only priests who have no faith in the real presence of our LORD in the Eucharist could be so uncaring.

In the *Constitutions* of the Fourth Lateran Council, held in 1215, in Paragraph 20, entitled: *On keeping the Chrism and the Eucharist under lock and key*, the Fathers of the said council state the following:

> "We decree that the Chrism and the Eucharist are to be kept locked away in a safe place in all churches, so that no audacious hand can reach them to do anything horrible or impious. If he who is responsible for their safe-keeping leaves them around carelessly, let him be suspended from office for three months; if anything unspeakable happens on account of his carelessness, let him be subject to graver punishment."[57]

This text shows a very profound concern of the Fathers of the Fourth Lateran Council for the protection of the Chrism and the Eucharist. They were very strict about the protection of the Eucharist, and those who did

---

[57] Ibid., *vol. I*, op. cit., p. 244.

not keep the Eucharist locked away in a safe place, but left it around carelessly, were to be suspended from office for three months, and if anything unspeakable happened on account of their carelessness, they were subject to graver punishment. Where are the penalties in the Church today? The Eucharistic Jesus is not only being left unprotected, but He is even brutally being profaned! And how many priests were suspended from office for this crime? I don't know of even one of them, but I know countless priests who profane the Eucharist. That's scandalous!

The associate pastor of the above-mentioned parish also informed me that the left-over Blood of Christ was being reposed in the tabernacle after the Sunday Masses and then, during the week, was being consumed by him little by little when he celebrated Mass. He and his pastor did not know that only the Consecrated Bread may be reposed in the tabernacle, whereas the Consecrated Wine must be immediately and completely consumed during Mass in accordance with what is written in Paragraph 279 of the *General Instruction of the Roman Missal*:

> "Care must be taken that whatever may remain of the Blood of Christ after the distribution of Communion is consumed immediately and completely at the altar."[58]

The only case when the Consecrated Wine may be reposed in the tabernacle is for a sick person. This rule has been confirmed by the United States Conference of Catholic Bishops in the document, entitled: *Norms for the Distribution and Reception of Holy Communion Under Both Kinds*

---

[58] *General Instruction of the Roman Missal*, op. cit., p. 93; see also Paragraph 163, p. 66.

in the Dioceses of the United States of America, approved in Rome at the Apostolic See on March 22, 2002 by the Congregation for Divine Worship and Discipline of the Sacraments. The content of this document is included in the *Roman Missal*, published in 2011. In Norm 54 of the said document, it is stated as follows:

> "The Precious Blood may not be reserved, except for giving Communion to someone who is sick. Only sick people who are unable to receive Communion under the form of bread may receive it under the form of wine alone at the discretion of the Priest. If not consecrated at a Mass in the presence of the sick person, the Blood of the LORD is kept in a properly covered vessel and is placed in the tabernacle after Communion. The Precious Blood should be carried to the sick in a vessel that is closed in such a way as to eliminate all danger of spilling. If some of the Precious Blood remains after the sick person has received Communion, it should be consumed by the minister, who should also see to it that the vessel is properly purified."[59]

According to this regulation, only sick people, who are unable to receive Holy Communion under the form of the Consecrated Bread, may receive the Eucharist under the form of the Consecrated Wine alone. Thus, in the case of sick people, who receive the Eucharist *outside* Mass, the Church recommends Holy Communion under the form of the Consecrated Bread alone, whereas Holy Communion under the form of the Consecrated

---

[59] *The Roman Missal* (New Jersey 2011), p. 85*.

Wine is reserved only for those who are unable to receive Holy Communion under the form of the Consecrated Bread. This restriction has been introduced by the Church for a practical reason, in order to prevent the Most Precious Eucharistic Blood of Christ from being accidentally spilled.

At this point, it is important to note that the Roman-Catholic Church generally recommends for lay people the receiving of Holy Communion under the form of the *Consecrated Bread alone*, and this is confirmed by both the Second Vatican Council and Canon Law itself. However, there are some theologians and priests who insist on the distribution of Holy Communion under both kinds for lay people, and they try to justify their position by referring to Paragraph 55 of the aforementioned *Constitution on the Sacred Liturgy* "Sacrosanctum Concilium" of the Second Vatican Council, promulgated on December 4, 1963, at its Session 3. The said Paragraph 55 reads as follows:

> "It is strongly encouraged that the people take part in the Mass more fully by receiving the Body of the LORD, after the priest's Communion, from the same Sacrifice as that from which he has received. Without in any way retracting the dogmatic principles laid down by the Council of Trent, Communion under both kinds may be allowed at the discretion of bishops, both to clergy and religious, and to lay people, in cases to be determined by the Apostolic See. Examples might be: people being ordained during the Mass of their ordination, people being professed in the Mass of their religious profession, and people who

have been newly baptized in the Mass following on their Baptism."[60]

The above-adduced text clearly states that the Eucharist under both kinds "may be allowed" in the Roman-Catholic Church. The Fathers of the Second Vatican Council do not say that Holy Communion "is to be" distributed to and received by lay people under both kinds. In the Roman-Catholic Church, the Eucharist under both kinds is not mandatory, but facultative. Thus, the first option, which the Roman-Catholic Church prefers, is the distribution and reception of the Eucharist by lay people under the form of the *Consecrated Bread alone*. By saying that "Communion under both kinds may be allowed," the Church *only* informs the faithful that such a possibility exists in the Roman-Catholic Church; the Church *only* gives permission for Communion under both kinds, but this does not mean that the Apostolic See recommends or encourages lay people to receive the Eucharist under both kinds. As with the Tridentine Mass, the Church *only* allows priests to celebrate the Tridentine Mass, but this does not mean that the Tridentine Mass should be celebrated on a regular basis; the celebration of the Tridentine Mass is *only* a possibility, but not a general liturgical rule in the Roman-Catholic Church. Those theologians and priests who claim that the Second Vatican Council recommends Holy Communion under both kinds for lay people must carefully read what the said council teaches. They should not make a universal rule out of the second option or possibility which the Church permits, because, in this way, they over-interpret the statements of the Church, promoting their far-fetched interpretations

---

[60] N. P. Tanner, *vol. II*, op. cit., p. 831.

which serve to justify their own concepts and visions. Such an attitude has nothing to do with professionalism. This is not fair; this is simply cheating!

The position of the Roman-Catholic Church on the issue of the distribution and reception of the Eucharist by lay people has been restated in Canon 925 of the *Code of Canon Law* which reads as follows:

> "Holy Communion is to be given *under the form of bread alone* [*sub sola specie panis*] or under both kinds in accord with the norm of the liturgical laws or even under the form of wine alone in case of necessity."[61]

Again, *Canon Law* plainly affirms, following Paragraph 55 of the *Constitution on the Sacred Liturgy* "Sacrosanctum Concilium" of the Second Vatican Council, that the first option, which the Roman-Catholic Church prefers, is the distribution and reception of the Eucharist by lay people under the form of the *Consecrated Bread alone*, whereas the Eucharist under both kinds is the second choice. Thus, Canon Law reinforces the statement of the Second Vatican Council, concerning the Eucharist for lay people. Many pastors who introduced the distribution of Holy Communion under both species kept and keep saying that the intention of the Roman-Catholic Church is that the faithful should receive the Eucharist under both species, but that is not what the ecclesiastical documents actually recommend. Canon 925 of the *Code of Canon Law* only states that "Holy Communion is to be given under the form of bread alone or under both kinds." Here, the mode of the conjunction: "or" is not recommendatory, but optional. By the way, Canon 925 also says that "Holy Communion is

---

[61] *Code of Canon Law*, op. cit., p. 345.

to be given under the form of bread alone [...] or even under the form of wine alone in case of necessity." The fact that Holy Communion may be allowed "under the form of wine alone in case of necessity" does not mean at all that the Roman-Catholic Church recommends and/ or encourages the faithful to receive the Eucharist "under the form of wine alone," but only "in case of necessity." Similarly, according to the quoted above *Constitution on the Sacred Liturgy* "Sacrosanctum Concilium" of the Second Vatican Council, "Communion under both kinds may be allowed at the discretion of bishops, both to clergy and religious, and to lay people, in cases to be determined by the Apostolic See. Examples might be: people being ordained during the Mass of their ordination, people being professed in the Mass of their religious profession, and people who have been newly baptized in the Mass following on their Baptism." Thus, the distribution of the Eucharist under both kinds for the laity is not the common, universal, normative rule in the Roman-Catholic Church, but it "may be allowed at the discretion of bishops" on some special occasions, not on a regular basis, for instance: "people being ordained during the Mass of their ordination, people being professed in the Mass of their religious profession, and people who have been newly baptized in the Mass following on their Baptism." As presented above, the Roman-Catholic Church unequivocally favors Holy Communion for lay people given under the form of the *Consecrated Bread alone*. This is also the manner the Eucharist is given when the Pope celebrates Holy Mass, and we should follow this pattern, especially during Sunday Masses.

I have never seen any official ecclesial document in which the Apostolic See would itself recommend and/ or encourage the distribution of Holy Communion under both forms during *Sunday Masses* on a regular basis, when many people gather together for the liturgy. It is not the intention of the Apostolic See that the Eucharist should be distributed under both forms during *Sunday Masses*, because if it were, then the Eucharist would be distributed under both kinds during *Sunday Masses* at the Vatican, but it is not. Such practice would be very burdensome. However, the distribution of Holy Communion under both forms during *Sunday Masses*, even with a large number of the faithful, has unfortunately become a *habitual* practice in North America, because the vast majority of the clergy does not want to follow the way of the Apostolic See. The Eucharist under both species, distributed during *Sunday Masses*, when usually many people come for the liturgy, suggests a lack of prudence and common sense. It is true that the distribution of Holy Communion under both kinds during *Sunday Masses* is not prohibited by the Apostolic See, but it is also true that the Apostolic See does not recommend nor encourage the distribution of this Most Blessed Sacrament under both forms during *Sunday Masses* attended by many people.

Once I participated at Mass in a diocese which celebrated the 150th anniversary of its existence. It was summertime, and over 30,000 people gathered in a park for Holy Mass during which the Eucharist was distributed under both species! The wine was consecrated in big flagons and *then* poured into very many glasses. Now, there are three very important observations which must be noted.

Firstly, the official Apostolic document, entitled: "Instruction on the Eucharist *Redemptionis Sacramentum*: On Certain Matters to Be Observed or to Be Avoided Regarding the Most Holy Eucharist," which was issued by the Congregation for Divine Worship and the Discipline of the Sacraments on March 25, 2004, prohibits the distribution of the Eucharist under both kinds for so vast a crowd. In Paragraph 101 of the said instruction *Redemptionis Sacramentum*, the following is commanded:

> "Holy Communion under both kinds [...] is to be completely excluded where even a small danger exists of the sacred species being profaned."[62]

The number of over 30,000 people, present at the above-mentioned Mass, speaks for itself that there did exist, not a small, but a great danger of the sacred species being profaned, and that's what actually happened.

Secondly, the Roman-Catholic Church prohibits the use of glass for the Eucharist, and especially for the Consecrated Wine. This juridical regulation is also contained in the afore-mentioned ecclesiastical document *Redemptionis Sacramentum* where it is said in Paragraph 106:

> "Never to be used for containing the Blood of the LORD are flagons, bowls, or other vessels that are not fully in accord with the established norms."[63]

Thirdly, the Blood of Christ is *never* poured from one chalice into another as it is also stated in the same Paragraph 106:

> "However, the pouring of the Blood of Christ after the consecration from one vessel to another is completely to be

---

[62] Instruction on the Eucharist *Redemptionis Sacramentum*: On Certain Matters to Be Observed or to Be Avoided Regarding the Most Holy Eucharist (Washington, D.C. 2004), p. 48.

[63] Ibid., p. 49.

avoided, lest anything should happen that would be to the detriment of so great a mystery."[64]

Accordingly, if many chalices are to be used, the wine is to be poured into them *before*, and *never after* the consecration. The worse thing, during the earlier mentioned Mass with over 30,000 people, was that due to the carelessness of the ministers of the Eucharist, who poured the Consecrated Wine from the flagons into the chalices, the altar-cloth was completely wet and pink in color. The altar was dripping with the Most Precious Blood of our LORD. There were many extraordinary Eucharistic ministers, and some of them were dressed in a suggestive, undignified manner. Most of the people did not choose to receive the Eucharist under both forms, but the ministers, who distributed Holy Communion, kept roaming among the people and asking them: "Do you want to drink wine?" "Do you want to drink wine?" The whole scene was senseless and awful to watch. A great amount of the Consecrated Wine remained after the distribution of the Eucharist had been finished. My heart was numb. I tried to do my best; I drank one big chalice of the Blood of Christ, and I felt inebriated. In my estimation, over two gallons of the Consecrated Wine still remained after the Mass. Did they consume it? Surely not. It is beyond any doubt that the Most Precious Blood of Christ was poured into the ground, just as it was the customary practice in that diocese. "Thus, Innocent Blood was [not] spared that day" (Daniel 13:62b). On that day, the wrath of God rested upon all those who were accountable for the profanation of the Eucharist. First of all, they did not protect the Eucharist, and secondly, they did not follow the rules of the Roman-Catholic Church. The Church does not permit the

---

[64] Ibid.

distribution of the Eucharist under both forms when a very large crowd of people participates in the Mass, and in this particular case the crowd was huge. At this point, a question arises: How would the Fathers of the afore-mentioned Council of Constance deal today not only with the practice of distributing the Eucharist under both species to the faithful on a regular basis every weekend, but above all how would they react to the fact that this Most Holy Sacrament is being so brutally profaned? The answer to this question can be one and only one, namely, they would unanimously, univocally and unequivocally condemn this evil practice, and all the abusers of the Eucharist would be declared heretics and effectively excommunicated. However, today there is little execution of the law of the Church, or it is executed very timidly. Such timidity has helped to create this immense and monstrous disorder and chaos in the very bosom of the Roman-Catholic Church for which God will punish us.

Many Catholics who demand the Eucharist under both species do not really understand the very nature of the Eucharist, thinking that when they receive the Consecrated Bread, they receive only the Body of Christ and when they receive the Consecrated Wine, they receive only the Blood of Christ. Accordingly, they believe that they "fully" participate in the Eucharist only when they receive it under both forms. Surprisingly and shockingly, such a perception of the Eucharist is represented even by some priests. I remember well how at a parish, in which I served, my pastor decided to introduce the distribution of the Most Holy Communion under both species. Prior to that, he made the following announcement: "Next weekend, we will begin in our parish the distribution of the Eucharist under both species, because we want the people to participate 'fully' in the Sacrament of the Body and Blood of Christ." I could not believe what I heard. To my greater surprise, this priest had a Ph.D. in dogmatic theology, and still more ironically, he wrote his doctoral dissertation on the theme: "Unless you eat the Flesh of the Son of Man and drink His Blood, you have no life in you" (John 6:53b). If a priest who accomplished his doctorate on a Biblical text pertaining to the Eucharist fails so fundamentally in the knowledge and understanding of the Sacrament of Holy Communion, then what can we expect from lay people who have never professionally studied theology? No wonder that so many lay people have a wrong perception of the nature of the Eucharist and many of them believe that everyone should receive Holy Communion under the form of the Consecrated Bread and under the form of the Consecrated Wine in order to participate "fully" in the Eucharist.

As a matter of fact, it is impossible to receive Jesus Christ in the Eucharist "partially," since in Holy Communion, He is undivided, and speaking still more precisely, He is indivisible. Consequently, the one who receives only the Consecrated Bread does not receive anything less than the one who receives the Eucharist under the form of the Consecrated Bread and under the form of the Consecrated Wine; in turn, the one who receives the Eucharist under both forms does not receive anything more than the one who receives only the Consecrated Bread. In short, we do not receive Jesus Christ "partially" when we receive the Eucharist under one form, because, as it has already been quoted earlier, the Council of Trent teaches that "Christ exists *whole* and *entire* under the form of bread and under any part of that form, and likewise *whole* under the form of wine and under its parts."[65]

---

[65] N. P. Tanner, *vol. II*, op. cit., p. 695.

Now, I want to explain very briefly why the receiving of the Most Holy Eucharist under both species is absolutely unnecessary by using a pictorial example. Let us say that someone goes to a doctor who prescribes for him two tablets of a medicine. However, the patient asks the doctor to prescribe for him the same medicine, but in liquid form. What is the difference? None, because the substance is 100% the same. And so, the receiving of the Eucharist under both forms could be compared to a patient who instead of taking his medicine in two tablets, or in two spoons, takes one tablet and one spoon of the same qualitative medicine.

At this point, it must also be stated that indeed "Holy Communion has a fuller form as a sign when it takes place under both kinds."[66] However, as regards the *very substance* of Holy Communion, each of its kinds, that is, the Consecrated Bread and the Consecrated Wine, absolutely equally embody the totally complete, undivided and indivisible *substance* of the Eucharistic LORD. The essence of the matter is that absolutely nothing is lacking in the Consecrated Bread, as well as absolutely nothing is lacking in the Consecrated Wine; they differ only in their forms, but not *in their qualitative substance*. Although the forms are different, the *substance* of both forms, that is, the *substance* of the Consecrated Bread and the *substance* of the Consecrated Wine is one and the same, one and absolutely the same. Consequently, it is totally wrong to believe that the *substance* of the Consecrated Bread and the *substance* of the Consecrated Wine have to "supplement each other" in order to constitute the "complete substance" of the Eucharist. But unfortunately there are more and more Catholics who think that they participate "fully" in the Eucharist only when they receive it under both species. They are not even aware that such an understanding

---

[66] *The Roman Missal*, op. cit., p. 81*.

of the Sacrament of Holy Communion questions the *oneness*, the *completeness* and the *perfection* of both the *substance* of the Consecrated Bread and the *substance* of the Consecrated Wine, because, according to this wrong concept, these two forms attain their "perfection" only when they are "supplemented by each other." But as it truly is, both the *substance* of the Consecrated Bread and the *substance* of the Consecrated Wine are equally perfect *in themselves*, each and individually; although in two forms, they are absolutely one and only one *in their qualitative essence*. In other words, the fullness and perfection of the *substance* of the Consecrated Bread do not depend on the *substance* of the Consecrated Wine, as well as the fullness and perfection of the *substance* of the Consecrated Wine do not depend on the *substance* of the Consecrated Bread. Therefore, from the theological point of view, it is impossible to assume that both the *substance* of the Consecrated Bread and the *substance* of the Consecrated Wine need a "mutual supplementation" so as to form the "full" and "perfect substance" of the Eucharistic Jesus Christ. Such interpretation of Holy Communion is pure heresy! It is absolutely true that "Holy Communion has a fuller form as a sign when it takes place under both kinds." However, the expression: "a fuller form as a sign" does not mean at all: "a fuller substance." Indeed, Holy Communion under both kinds "has a fuller form as a sign," inasmuch as in the Upper Room, our LORD consecrated both bread and wine, but as regards the *Eucharistic substance itself*, both the Consecrated Bread and the Consecrated Wine, each of them individually and together, are the *full substance* of the Eucharistic Jesus Christ. Therefore, the above-mentioned Ecumenical Council of Trent teaches, in Chapter 3 of its *Decree on the Most Holy Sacrament of the Eucharist*, entitled: *On the excellence of the*

Most Holy Eucharist over the other sacraments, formulated at its Session 13, held on October 11, 1551, as follows:

> "The Body is present under the form of bread and the Blood under the form of wine, by virtue of the Words. The same Body, however, is under the form of wine and the Blood under the form of bread [...]. Hence it is entirely true that as much is contained under one of the forms as under both; for Christ exists whole and entire under the form of bread and under any part of that form, and likewise whole under the form of wine and under its parts."[67]

Accordingly, when a priest utters the Words of Consecration over the bread, the Consecrated Bread does not contain only the Body of Christ, but both the Body and the Blood of Christ, although the priest did not use the term: "blood;" likewise, when he utters the Words of Consecration over the wine, the Consecrated Wine does not contain only the Blood of Christ, but both the Blood and the Body of Christ, although the priest did not use the term: "body." At this point, we must also note another very important issue, namely, in the entire formula of the consecration, be it the words over the bread and/ or over the wine, the priest does not say anything about the Soul nor about the Divinity of our LORD Jesus Christ, but as it truly is, both His Human Soul and His Divinity are present in Holy Communion. What is not said *expressis verbis* in the Words of Consecration themselves is *logically* and *theologically* deduced from the very fact that the *entire* LORD, *undivided* and *indivisible*, is present in every, absolutely every,

---

[67] N. P. Tanner, *vol. II*, op. cit., p. 695.

even the smallest particle of the Eucharist. The Blessed Sacrament of the Body and Blood of Jesus Christ is a GREAT MYSTERY which surpasses our human, limited imagination, but our *logical* and *theological* discernment, as well as our faith come to our aid thanks to "the Spirit of Truth" (1 John 4:6d; 5:6c), "the Spirit of God [who] dwells in [us]" (1 Corinthians 3:16; cf. James 4:5b), and who gives us Divine Life (cf. 2 Corinthians 3:6b). It is also thanks to the Holy Spirit, acting in the Church, that "we have the same spirit of faith" (2 Corinthians 4:13a), if we only accept and obey the *collective, ecclesiastical* spirit of faith which is guarded and cherished by the Office of the Magisterium of the Roman-Catholic Church, that is, by its authoritative Office of Teaching in the Name of God. "Therefore, he who rejects this does not reject man, but God who has also given us His Holy Spirit" (1 Thessalonians 4:8), living "in us who do not walk according to the flesh, but according to the Spirit" (Romans 8:4), "if indeed the Spirit of God dwells in [us]" (Romans 8:9a). "These things God has revealed to us through the Spirit; for the Spirit searches everything, even the depths of God" (1 Corinthians 2:10), and if so, then the Spirit of God searches also the depths of the Eucharistic Mystery and reveals them to us, inasmuch as "no one knows the things of God except the Spirit of God" (1 Corinthians 2:11b). "Now we have received not the spirit of the world, but the Spirit who is from God, that we might understand the things that have been freely bestowed on us by God" (1 Corinthians 2:12).

Having in mind all that has been said in the above paragraph, we must state that when a priest distributes the Eucharist to the faithful and says: "The Body of Christ," it does not mean at all that a person receives only the Body of Christ, and when he says: "The Blood of Christ," it does not mean at all that a person receives only the Blood of Christ. When a priest gives the Consecrated Bread, saying: "The Body of Christ," a person receives both the Body and the Blood of Christ, as well as when he gives the Consecrated Wine, saying: "The Blood of Christ," a person receives both the Blood and the Body of Christ, because in Holy Communion it is impossible to separate the *Eucharistic* Body from the *Eucharistic* Blood of Christ. Such a separation was possible *only* in the life of the *historical Jesus*, but it is impossible in the *Sacramental Mystery of the Eucharistic LORD* in which He is present whole and entire: *Body* and *Blood*, *Soul* and *Divinity*, in every, even the smallest, part of the Most Holy Communion, be it the Consecrated Bread and/ or the Consecrated Wine.

There were many Catholics, in the past, who supported the distribution of Holy Communion under both species, and there are also many today who insist on this practice, saying: "This is the way the Eucharist should be received by the People of God." Of course, from the theological viewpoint, the distribution of Holy Communion under both forms is unquestionably correct; however, along with theological correctness, we must also have a correct pastoral leadership and practice. But if the distribution of the Eucharist under both species opens an opportunity to its abuse, then it should instantly be terminated, and distributed under the form of the Consecrated Bread alone which is also unquestionably correct, from the theological point of view, as the receiving of the Eucharist under both kinds.

Whether or not a practice is pastorally good can best be evaluated from the fruit it yields. And what is the outcome of this practice? The distribution of the Eucharist under both species neither has increased the faith of the People of God nor has it sanctified them, but on the contrary, it has brought about a mega problem in the Roman-Catholic Church, inasmuch as it has opened a way to an enormous abuse of this Most Holy Sacrament.

In this way, the spiritual condition of thousands of Catholics, who profaned the Most Precious Blood of our LORD, has turned from better to worse. What was to be a means of sanctification for Catholics has ironically become a means of their condemnation. During Mass, in the second prayer before receiving Holy Communion, every priest utters silently the following words from the *Roman Missal*: "May the receiving of your Body and Blood, LORD Jesus Christ, not bring me to judgment and condemnation, but through your loving mercy be for me protection in mind and body and a healing remedy."[68] Look for what the celebrant asks Jesus Christ. The receiving of the Eucharist can be a healing remedy or it can bring judgment and condemnation. In other words, the receiving of the Eucharist can be a spiritual healer or killer. The Eucharist heals those who approach it with faith and reverence, but the same Eucharist kills those who profane it. The fruit of receiving the Eucharist depends on our spiritual condition, whether or not we are properly disposed towards it. If we receive Holy Communion with a pure heart, then it is for us a healing remedy, but if we receive the Eucharist in the condition of mortal sin, that is to say, sacrilegiously, then, the Eucharist brings judgment and condemnation. How much more does the Eucharist bring judgment and condemnation upon those who profane it by pouring the Most Sacred Blood of Jesus Christ into the sacrarium. The Author of the Letter to the Hebrews writes: "Anyone who has rejected Moses' Law dies without mercy on the testimony of two or three witnesses. How much worse punishment, do you think, will he deserve who has trampled under foot the Son of God, profaned the Blood of the Covenant by which he was sanctified, and has insulted the Spirit of Grace? For we know Him who said: 'Vengeance is Mine, I will repay'

---

[68] *The Roman Missal*, op. cit., p. 520.

[...]. And again, 'the LORD will judge His people.' It is a fearful thing to fall into the hands of the Living God" (Hebrews 10:28–31). We can see how timely are these words even today in the face of the profanation of the Most Holy Blood of Christ. The Eucharistic Jesus is this Most Precious Gift from God the Father who sanctifies and enlightens those who receive Him with faith and love, but those who profane the Eucharist fall into the deep darkness of mortal sin.

Many priests believed that the distribution of Holy Communion under both forms was a right service in the Church, but in practice they lacked wisdom and prudence. The Wisdom of God says on the pages of Sacred Scripture that "the multitude of the wise is the salvation of the world, and a prudent king is the stability of his people" (Wisdom 6:24). These words can be adapted to every Roman-Catholic priest who is in charge of a pastoral service; he is to be guided by wisdom and prudence which God reveals in the Bible and through the Authorities of the Roman-Catholic Church. Unfortunately many unlearned priests have destabilized the People of God by profaning the Most Precious Blood of our LORD Jesus Christ, because they did not draw their spiritual and pastoral inspirations from Divine Wisdom, but did follow their own designs which were contrary to the will of God and the will of His Holy Church. Sacred Scripture says: "Prudence renders service" (Wisdom 8:6). However, a lack of prudence, on the part of so many undisciplined and liberal priests, has rendered spiritual disaster for so many Catholics. The distribution of the Eucharist under both species only seemed to be a right pastoral decision, but, in effect, it soon turned out to be a tragic failure and a fiasco for those priests who had no sense of pastoral wisdom and of common sense. An apt comment on this situation can be found in the Book of Proverbs which reads as follows: "There is a way that seems right to a man, but its end is the way of death" (Proverbs 14:12: exactly the same statement is repeated in 16:25). How perfectly the above-adduced words fit the problem in question. It seemed to many priests and lay people as well that the distribution of the Eucharist under both species would benefit Catholics, but in reality it worsened their spiritual condition. The distribution of the Eucharist under both forms has engendered a massive profanation of this Most Holy Sacrament, leading many Catholics to a spiritual ruin, to a spiritual death. Those priests who introduced the distribution of the Eucharist under both kinds lacked prudence, being very short-sighted (cf. 2 Peter 1:9). Now, to have pastoral prudence and foresight is part of being a good and trustworthy shepherd (cf. 1 Corinthians 4:2), and, needless to say, many are not. Therefore, today's Church suffers bitterly, because so many "amateur" priests have no clue about mature ministry in the Church.

The Council of Constance states in its opening sentence at Session 14, held on July 4, 1415, that "the most important part of any matter is its beginning."[69] How true this is in the case of the distribution of the Eucharist under both species in North America. From the *pastoral* and *practical* perspectives, the introduction of Holy Communion under both species was wrong from the very beginning, because this practice started without any solid prior theological and canonical preparation, and those from among the clergy, who did not know what to do with the remaining Blood of Christ, were pouring it into the sacrarium, saying: "That's what the sacrarium is for." This totally false interpretation has quickly spread from diocese to diocese and infected countless priests, deacons and extraordinary Eucharistic

---

[69] N. P. Tanner, *vol. I*, op. cit., p. 420.

ministers, and this gangrene consumes the Roman-Catholic Church in North America until today.

The profanation of the Most Holy Eucharist has germinated with the increase of *doctrinal*, *liturgical* and *disciplinary* errors when liberal and unlearned priests have introduced the practice of the distribution of the Eucharist under both species by their own whim. This practice antedated, in many parishes throughout North America, the official permission of the Authorities of the Roman-Catholic Church. And since those who began to distribute the Eucharist under both kinds did not know what to do with the remaining Blood of Christ, they contrived the wrong theory presuming that the Blood of Christ is allegedly to be poured into the sacrarium. All those who forced this illicit, erroneous and demonic practice proved themselves to be very immature, false and blind shepherds in the sheep-fold of Christ (cf. 2 Peter 1:9). They lacked not only a solid priestly education, but first of all, first and foremost and above all, they lacked – faith, because everyone who believes in the real presence of our LORD in Holy Communion wants to protect the Eucharistic Jesus as much as possible, and it is obvious that the Consecrated Wine needs a more careful service than the Consecrated Bread for the simple reason that it is liquid.

As it has been explained above, everyone who knows the nature of the Eucharist understands that it is unnecessary to receive it under both forms, but, what I observe, the less theologically mature a person is, the more he insists on receiving Holy Communion under both species. There is no doubt that for all the years, and to be more precisely for all the decades, during which the Eucharist has been distributed under both forms, the People of God have not become holier at all, but the spiritual condition of thousands of Catholics has turned from better to worse because of the profanation of this Most Blessed Sacrament. As I see it, this crime can be stopped most efficiently by an official prohibition of the distribution of the Eucharist under both species because of so many faithless and careless people in the Church who have no sense of sacredness in dealing with the Most Holy Communion and act as barbarians, "for not all have faith" (2 Thessalonians 3:2b). Let us be always mindful of the words of our LORD Jesus Christ who has said: "Do not give what is holy to dogs, and do not throw your pearls before swine, lest they trample them under their feet, and turn and tear you to pieces" (Matthew 7:6). Therefore, those who have no sense of *Sacrum* and who do not believe in the real presence of Jesus Christ in the Eucharist should not have access to this Most Holy Sacrament. With sacred things, one must deal prudently that they be not desecrated. However, those who profane the Eucharist trample the Most Precious Pearls of the Body and Blood of Christ under their feet. In this manner, they turn not only against God Himself, but also against His faithful people when they scandalize them by this sacrilegious practice; they tear our LORD into pieces (cf. Psalm 22:17c; 35:15c), and simultaneously, they tear into pieces the faith of the People of God in the Eucharist.

In his opening address at the Fifth Lateran Council, at Session 2, held on May 17, 1512, Pope Julius II said: "We intend, with the help of the Most High, to proceed with the holding of this sacred Lateran Council which has now begun for the praise of God, the peace of the whole Church, the union of the faithful, the overthrow of heresies and schisms, the reform of morals, and the campaign against the dangerous enemies of the faith, so that the mouths of all schismatics and enemies of peace, those howling dogs, may be silenced and Christians may be able to keep themselves unstained from such pernicious and poisonous contagion."[70] What we need today is for the above-quoted words of Pope Julius II to be uttered anew against all those "howling dogs" who have created this "pernicious and poisonous contagion" which is the profanation of the Eucharist, and which *interiorly* consumes the Mystical Body of the Roman-Catholic Church. They tear holes in the Most Holy Body of our LORD Jesus Christ who complains together with the Psalmist, saying: "Dogs have surrounded Me; the congregation of the wicked has enclosed Me. They have pierced My hands and My feet" (Psalm 22:17). My Blood has been "poured out like water" (Psalm 22:15a). They "have brought Me to the dust of death" (Psalm 22:16b). The Apostle Paul also writes in his Letter to the Philippians: "Beware of the dogs, beware of the evil workers" (Philippians 3:2) who, in the Book of Revelation, belong to those who are outside the Holy City of the Heavenly Jerusalem (cf. Revelation 22:15). And in his Second Letter to the Corinthians, the same Apostle warns us of "false apostles [and] deceitful workers" (2 Corinthians 11:13). There is no doubt that those priests who willfully profane the Eucharist are false apostles and deceitful workers who – according to Canon Law and the Instruction *Redemptionis Sacramentum* – have incurred the penalty of excommunication, and *ipso facto* have placed themselves outside the Church, since that's what excommunication brings about. They act madly to their own and others' ruin, splitting asunder the unity of our Holy Mother Church (cf. the Fifth Lateran Council, at Session 3 held on December 3, 1512).[71]

Those who profane the Most Holy Eucharist are false prophets who spread the culture of spiritual death, because that is what the consequence

---

[70] Ibid., p. 595.
[71] Cf. ibid., p. 597.

of this terrible abuse is all about: *excommunication* is a *spiritual death*. Jesus Christ has said: "Beware of false prophets, who come to you in sheep's clothing, but inwardly they are ravenous wolves. You will know them by their fruits. Do men gather grapes from thornbushes or figs from thistles? Even so, every good tree bears good fruit, but a bad tree bears bad fruit. A good tree cannot bear bad fruit, nor can a bad tree bear good fruit. Every tree that does not bear good fruit is cut down and thrown into the fire. Therefore, by their fruits you will know them" (Matthew 7:15–20; cf. 12:33–35; Luke 6:43–45). And what is the fruit of those priests who profane the Most Holy Eucharist? It is an *excommunication*! The prediction of the appearance of false prophets has also been foretold by Saint Paul the Apostle in Miletus, where he addressed the elders of the church from Ephesus (cf. Acts 20:17) in the following words: "Therefore take heed to yourselves and to all the flock, among which the Holy Spirit has made you overseers, to shepherd the Church of God which He purchased with His own blood. For I know this, that after my departure savage wolves will come in among you, not sparing the flock. Also from among yourselves men will rise up, speaking perverse things, to draw away the disciples after themselves. Therefore, watch, and remember that for three years I did not cease to warn everyone night and day with tears" (Acts 20:28–31). In the history of the Church, the words of Saint Paul fulfilled themselves many times in the past and they also fulfill themselves in our times. Indeed, those who desecrate the Eucharist are, beyond any doubt, savage wolves among the sheep of Christ who do not spare His flock. Because of this disgraceful crime, they are deprived of the Grace of God, being spiritually unfed and empty just as Saint John Chrysostom says in a homily on the Gospel according to Saint Matthew, namely, that our Divine Shepherd "feeds the sheep not wolves."[72] All those priests who *habitually* profane the Eucharist rebel against God, and therefore, they are spiritually eviscerated, for they do not fulfill, in their Christian and priestly life, the will of God. Jesus Christ says in the Gospel of Saint John: "My food is to do the will of Him who sent Me, and to finish His work" (John 4:34b). If the fulfillment of the will of His Heavenly Father was for our Divine and Life-giving Master Himself His spiritual food, how much more we, who are human and mortal, need to be fed on the will of God so as to live in friendship with God on earth and to be partakers of His Eternal Glory in Heaven. The point is that everyone who willfully resists the will of God simultaneously follows the will of the devil, and is fed on the poisonous and deadly food of eternal condemnation. This is the destiny of all those who, imitating satan, perversely act against the will of God. And what can be more perverse, mutinous, seditious and murderous than to raise one's hand against Jesus Christ really present in the Most Holy Eucharist. This is an obvious act of anarchy against our LORD Jesus Christ which has been introduced by so many rebellious priests in the very bosom of the Roman-Catholic Church and which spreads as a pestilence throughout North America, because it was not suppressed immediately. Therefore, the core of the problem, concerning the profanation of the Eucharist, lies not only in the ignorance and arrogance of those priests who desecrate this Most Sacred Sacrament, but also in the negligence on the part of those bishops who, knowing about this crime, do not act promptly, being intimidated by the defiance and the aggressiveness of their pastors. The profanation of the Eucharist is so grave a sacramental abuse that every bishop who hears about it must react instantaneously;

---

[72] "From a homily on Matthew by Saint John Chrysostom, bishop," [in]: *The Liturgy of the Hours, vol. IV* (New York 1975), p. 599.

otherwise, he himself becomes an accomplice. Every act of the desecration of the Eucharist is a matter of utmost urgency which brooks no delay. Here, the words of Pope Eugenius IV are worthy of remembrance who, following Saint Jerome, addressed the Fathers of the Council of Florence at Session 9, held on March 23, 1440, saying among other things: "Arius[73] [...] was a spark in Alexandria but, because he was not immediately extinguished, his flame ravaged the whole world."[74] That is exactly the case with the profanation of the Eucharist. Had the priests who started the practice of pouring the Blood of Christ into the sacrarium been "immediately extinguished," the flame of this horrific crime would not have ravaged the Church. In his opening statement, at the same council and at the same session, Pope Eugenius IV also said: "Many examples of Holy Fathers of the Old and the New Testament warn us that we should not pass over in silence or leave completely unpunished specially grave crimes which lead to the scandal and public division of the people entrusted to us. For if we delay to pursue and avenge what is grievously offensive to God, we thereby provoke the Divine patience to wrath. For there are sins for which it is a sin to be slack about their retribution. It is indeed right and eminently reasonable, in the opinion of Holy Fathers, that those who despise Divine commands and disobey paternal enactments should be corrected with really severe penalties, so that others may fear to commit the same faults and that all may rejoice in fraternal harmony and take note of the example of severity and probity. For if – though may it never be – we are negligent about ecclesiastical

---

[73] Arius (ca. 250 – ca. 336) was a heresiarch who denied the Divinity of Christ. For his heresy, he was condemned and excommunicated at the First Ecumenical Council of Nicaea, held in 325; cf. F. L. Cross – E. A. Livingstone, op. cit., pp. 87.967.

[74] N. P. Tanner, *vol. I*, op. cit., p. 560.

vigilance and activity, idleness ruins discipline and the souls of the faithful will suffer great harm. Therefore, rotting flesh should be cut away and mangy sheep driven out of the flock, so that the whole body or flock may not be infected and perish. [...]

We have learnt from the example of Apostolic Authority that those who err and lead others into error are to be handed over to satan by ecclesiastical censures, so that their spirit may be saved (cf. 1 Corinthians 5:5) and others may learn not to blaspheme (cf. 1 Timothy 1:20) [...]. We understand that no other course is open to us than to bend our every effort against that cause by which the safety of the universal Church is threatened."[75] Needless to say how much we need to put into practice today the above-adduced words of His Holiness Eugenius IV, because sloth and idleness, pertaining to the desecration of the Most Holy Eucharist, devastate the Roman-Catholic Church from within to the spiritual detriment of so many Catholics.

As mentioned above, the sacrilegious practice of pouring the Most Holy Blood of Christ into the sacrarium has been going on for approximately a half century! Therefore, after such a long time of committing this "liturgical butchery," we are morally obliged "to rise to the defence of the Church and tackle this great crime more quickly and more urgently,"[76] using the language of the afore-said Pope Eugenius IV from his speech addressed to the Fathers of the Ecumenical Council of Florence at Session 9 held on March 23, 1440. We need to stop this terrible abuse in the very bosom of the Roman-Catholic Church with the least possible delay, offering a remedy[77] to the perpetrators in accordance with Canon Law and the Instruction

---

[75] Ibid., pp. 559–560.
[76] Ibid., p. 564.
[77] Cf. ibid.

Redemptionis Sacramentum, since God has "no pleasure in the death of the wicked, but that the wicked turn from his way and live" (Ezekiel 33:11b).

I had three private conversations with the ordinary of a large and influential diocese concerning the profanation of the Eucharist. This abuse took place all over his diocese for a long time even before his installation, including at the cathedral and in the seminary itself. Moreover, the seminarians were being taught falsely that the pouring of the Blood of Christ into the sacrarium was allegedly a legal practice of the Roman-Catholic Church. Ironically, the rector of that seminary – even before the installation of the said ordinary – was ordained an auxiliary bishop of the diocese in question, and later he himself was appointed as the ordinary of a diocese. One can only imagine how he leads his diocese.

I also know a rector from another diocese who, prior to his assignment to the seminary, allowed the profanation of the Eucharist in the largest parish of the diocese where he earlier worked as the pastor. I cannot conceive how such a priest can be responsible for the theological, spiritual and liturgical formation of seminarians. This poor priest must first carefully read Chapter 16 of the *Constitution on the Sacred Liturgy*, promulgated by the Second Vatican Council at its Session 3 held on December 4, 1963, which instructs as follows:

> "The subject of liturgy must be regarded in seminaries and in religious houses of study as a compulsory 'core' subject; in theology faculties, it is to be regarded as one of the principal areas of enquiry. It must be taught both theologically and historically, and also with regard to its spiritual, pastoral and juridical aspects. Moreover, teachers of other

branches of study, especially dogma, Scripture, spirituality and pastoral theology, should see that they give due respect to the mystery which is Christ and the history of salvation, against the background of the intrinsic demands of the subject-matter dealt with specifically by each of them. In this way, the connection between these subjects and the liturgy, and the underlying unity of priestly formation, will become self-evidently clear."[78]

Now let us return to the afore-mentioned bishop with whom I had three private conversations. Our first conversation took place just two months after his installation. The bishop condemned the profanation of the Eucharist in his diocese, saying: "This practice was wrong, and it must be stopped." Upon hearing this, I was very glad, but sadly ten months after the installation of the ordinary, I found out that the Blood of Christ was still being poured into the sacrarium in the very cathedral! When I informed the bishop about that, he said: "I must talk to the rector of the cathedral again." This is a classical example of how sometimes even a bishop may not know what is going on in his house. Finally, the bishop appointed a new rector who stopped the profanation of the Eucharist at the cathedral. However, this was just the tip of the iceberg. The sacrilegious practice of pouring the Precious Blood of Christ into the sacrarium continued in his diocese and still continues until today! When I had a third and the longest conversation with the said bishop, pertaining to the profanation of the Eucharist, I brought to his attention that this abuse was still taking place in his diocese. Hearing this he was surprised, but I was not

---

[78] Ibid., *vol. II*, p. 824–825.

surprised at all. Why? Because the bishop has never issued any pastoral letter by which he would unequivocally condemn and prohibit the pouring of the Eucharistic Blood of Jesus Christ into the sacrarium in his diocese, and I do not know what deterred him from doing this, presumably the fear of rebellious and aggressive clergy. He was only *privately* and *orally* correcting those who profaned the Eucharist, but to no avail. Moreover, the bishop did not show any, absolutely any concern for the excommunicated priests who needed absolution from the Apostolic See for their desecration of the Eucharist. Seeing this, I said to the bishop: "Please, save the priests who have profaned the Eucharist from going to hell, and seek for them an absolution from the Apostolic See." But he responded: "They are not excommunicated." In this manner, the bishop put himself over the law of the Roman-Catholic Church. However, the law of the Church is relentless, and those who profane the Eucharist *automatically* incur the penalty of *excommunication* reserved to the Apostolic See, or Canon Law and the Instruction *Redemptionis Sacramentum* are just a kind of juridical scarecrow. Even the enormously great number of the priests who desecrate the Most Sacred Eucharist cannot water down the regulations of the Roman-Catholic Church, just as the huge number of those who commit abortion is unable to change the teaching of the Church on this issue.

In our last conversation, the bishop informed me that he *personally* saw the copy of a letter which had been sent to all the priests of his diocese over 40 years ago in which the former authorities of the diocese falsely instructed the clergy to pour the left-over Blood of Christ into the sacrarium. This godless letter of a clearly criminal character has passed judgment on our LORD Jesus Christ. It is scandalous that this evil document was issued by the *Office of Divine Worship* of the said diocese, that it was the product of a collective decision, the outcome of a perverse counsel. But the Wisdom of God says that "inquiry will be made into the counsels of the ungodly, and a report of their words will come to the LORD, to convict them of their lawless deeds" (Wisdom 1:9). All the priests who worked for this office, at that time, were morally responsible for the disarray they created. They were called to serve Jesus Christ at His Altar *ex professo* and to be His subjects, but they put themselves over God and over the law of His Holy Church, acting like "arrogant giants" (Wisdom 14:6; cf. Baruch 3:26). As a consequence, they fell, losing the way of understanding (cf. Baruch 3:27), and now, they perish for lack of prudence, they perish through their folly (cf. Baruch 3:28), living in the state of excommunication, that is to say, living out of the Church of Jesus Christ, as a consequence of their treacherous plot against Him. Sacred Scripture reads that "perverse thoughts separate people from God, and when His power is tested, it exposes the foolish; because Wisdom will not enter a deceitful soul, or dwell in a body enslaved to sin" (Wisdom 1:3–4). "The crown of Wisdom is the fear of the LORD" (Sirach 1:18a; cf. Wisdom 3:15b). Again, "the fear of the LORD is the beginning of Wisdom" (Proverbs 9:10; Sirach 1:14a) and "the beginning of knowledge" (Proverbs 1:7), and "the knowledge of the Holy One is understanding" (Proverbs 9:10), "but fools despise Wisdom and instruction" (Proverbs 1:7). As Saint James the Apostle writes: "The Wisdom that is from above is first pure, then peaceable, gentle, willing to yield, full of mercy and good fruits, without partiality and without hypocrisy" (James 3:17).

Those who profane the Eucharist, and instruct others to do the same, lack the above-adduced virtues, but first of all they lack a fear of the LORD. The Bible says that "the fear of the LORD is Wisdom, and to depart from evil is understanding" (Job 28:28b). "Those who fear the LORD do not disobey His words, and those who love Him keep His ways" (Sirach 2:15); "those who fear the LORD seek to please Him, and those who love Him are filled with His Law" (Sirach 2:16). However, those who desecrate the Most Holy Eucharist lack Wisdom, because they do not fear the LORD; they lack understanding, because they do not depart from evil; they do not obey the words of God, taught by the Authorities of the Roman-Catholic Church, because they are demonically arrogant. Consequently, they are not filled with the Law of God, and they do not keep His ways, but walk their own ways of apostasy. The insolence of those who profane the Eucharist leads them to excommunication which is spiritual death; they do not attend to the voice of God's Wisdom that cries out: "Do not invite death by the error of your life, or bring on destruction by the works of your hands, because God did not make death, and he does not delight in the death of the living" (Wisdom 1:12–13).

It is very sad that the ordinary of the said diocese has never *officially* and *administratively* recanted the aforementioned diocesan letter which opened a way to the profanation of the Most Holy Eucharist on an enormous and unimaginable scale. This evil letter recalls a Biblical scene. In the Book of Esther, we find the story of the plot of Haman who was a powerful vizier of King Ahasuerus (Xerxes) of Persia (485–464 B.C.).[79] At that time, King Ahasuerus reigned from his royal throne in the citadel of Susa (cf. Esther 1:2). One day, King Ahasuerus raised Haman to high rank, seating him above all the princes of his kingdom (cf. Esther 3:1). As Sacred Scripture relates, "Haman sought to destroy all the Jews who were throughout the whole kingdom of Ahasuerus" (Esther 3:6b), and he said to King Ahasuerus: "There is a certain people scattered and dispersed among

---

[79] Cf. *The New American Bible* (New York 1970), p. 500.

the people in all the provinces of your kingdom; their laws are different from all other people's, and they do not keep the king's laws. Therefore, it is not fitting for the king to let them remain. If it pleases the king, let a decree be written that they be destroyed, and I will pay ten thousand talents of silver into the hands of those who do the work, to bring it into the king's treasuries" (Esther 3:8b–9). King Ahasuerus consented to the destruction of the Israelites; he "took his signet ring from his hand and gave it to Haman" (Esther 3:10). "Then the king's scribes were called on the thirteenth day of the first month, and a decree was written according to all that Haman commanded, to the king's satraps, to the governors who were over each province, to the officials of all people, to every province according to its script, and to every people in their language. In the name of King Ahasuerus it was written, and sealed with the king's signet ring. And the letters were sent by couriers into all the king's provinces, to destroy, to kill, and to annihilate all the Jews, both young and old, little children and women, in one day, on the thirteenth day of the twelfth month, which is the month of Adar, and to plunder their possessions. A copy of the decree was to be promulgated as law in every province, being published for all the peoples, that they should be ready for that day. The couriers set out in haste at the king's command; meanwhile, the decree was proclaimed in the stronghold of Susa. Then the king and Haman sat down to drink, but the city of Susa was thrown into confusion" (Esther 3:12–15).

Over 40 years ago, the former authorities of the diocese in question acted as King Ahasuerus and Haman; they issued a written document as their own law which, in fact, was pure lawlessness. As a consequence, the whole diocese has been thrown into confusion. The "Hamanites" of that diocese took the signet ring from their bishop, they wrote a letter in his name, and sealed it with the bishop's signet ring. Then the copies of the letter were sent to all the priests of the diocese to "legalize" lawlessly the criminal practice of crucifying our LORD Jesus Christ with impunity. In this way, the authorities of the diocese have established an organized crime against God Himself. This must be stated very strongly that the profanation of the Eucharist is a crime committed against our LORD, since the Most Holy Eucharist is – JESUS CHRIST HIMSELF. The Eucharist is NOT a symbol, but the Living and Life-giving Incarnate Son of God. As all the Israelites were to be exterminated in all the provinces of Ahasuerus' kingdom, so also Jesus was to be executed in all the parishes of the said diocese, where His Most Holy Blood was to be poured into the sacrarium. In both cases, this was done by an official letter, but with one essential difference, namely, the letter condemning all the Israelites to death was promulgated by pagans, but the letter of the said diocese was issued by those who according to the flesh are the brothers of Jesus Christ (cf. Romans 9:5).

As the Bible relates, God saved His people, but Haman was hung on the gibbet which he had prepared for Mordecai, a prominent Israelite, whom Haman hated (cf. Esther 7:9–10). The "gibbet" of those who profane the Eucharist is the penalty of excommunication which they have incurred through the profanation of the Eucharist, and they will "hang on it" as long as they do not repent and ask the Apostolic See for absolution. May the example of one of the criminals who was crucified along with Jesus help them all not to lose their souls. At the last moment of his life, the humbled and contrite criminal asked Jesus for His mercy, saying: "LORD, remember me, when you come into your Kingdom" (Luke 23:42b). And the Merciful LORD replied: "Truly I say to you, today you will be with Me in Paradise"

(Luke 23:43b). They should not waste their time, lest it be too late, but they should repent and be reconciled with God as soon as possible.

It is scandalous that the diocese in question issued an official diocesan document which totally contradicted the law of the Church, and "legalized" the lawless practice of crucifying our LORD Jesus Christ in the bosom of the Roman-Catholic Church. Shame on all those messengers of this bad, evil and devastating news! However, before the installation of the said ordinary, a zealous woman wrote to all the pastors of his diocese a letter in which she reminded them of Norm 38 of the *Directory for the Celebration and Reception of Communion under Both Kinds* promulgated by the Episcopal Conference of the United States on November 1, 1984. There was a group of priests who reacted positively to her initiative, but most of them responded with nasty and angry letters, and the profanation of the Eucharist continues in that diocese up to the present. So then, prior to the installation of the bishop, the priests of his diocese were fully aware that the pouring of the Blood of Christ into the sacrarium was strictly prohibited; nevertheless, they did not convert and, in their hardness of heart, they continued this demonic practice, whereas the ordinary remained shiftless, helpless and at a loss. The Bible says that "a wicked messenger falls into evil, but a faithful envoy is a healing remedy" (Proverbs 13:17). The above-mentioned faithful woman was, indeed, a healing remedy for the priests of her diocese, and she did much more in defense of the Eucharistic Jesus than the bishop. It is hard to believe, but such are the facts. The question arises: Who is to watch over the flock of Christ? The bishop received a Biblical talent from Jesus Christ, his LORD; however, he did not multiply his talent, but he gave it back to Jesus (cf. Matthew 25:14–15.18.24–30; Luke 19:12–13.20–24.27). May God bless this courageous woman! She is in one person both Mary and Martha (cf. Luke 10:38–42), because she not only sat at the LORD's feet and listened to His word (cf. Luke 10:39), but she was also moved by His word to action and waited on Him with a tender love. The ordinary of the said diocese did stop the profanation of the Eucharist at his seminary, but not in the parishes, with some few exceptions, because he was afraid of the rapacious clergy. However, even if the seminarians, in his diocese, are now properly instructed at the seminary, when they go to serve in different parishes, and when they are later ordained and assigned to the parishes, they face the desecration of the Eucharist and their pastors force them to continue this evil practice. Thus, a lack of manly courage, on the part of the bishop, keeps this mess going on even today, because the bishop did not pattern his ministry in the Church on the Sacrifice of our LORD Jesus Christ, being overcome by hopeless fear and forgetting the exhortation of Saint Paul the Apostle which he addressed to Timothy: "Fight the good fight of faith" (1 Timothy 6:12), "for God has not given us a spirit of fear, but of power and of love and of a sound mind" (2 Timothy 1:7). "You, therefore, must endure hardship as a good soldier of Jesus Christ" (2 Timothy 2:3). "Hold fast to the pattern of sound teaching [...]. Guard the good deposit, which was entrusted to you, by the Holy Spirit who dwells in us" (2 Timothy 1:13–14). "Take heed to yourself and to the doctrine; persevere at both tasks, for in doing this you will save both yourself and those who hear you" (1 Timothy 4:16). "Therefore, I remind you to stir up the gift of God which is in you through the laying on of my hands" (2 Timothy 1:6).

As mentioned above, there are bishops who know about the profanation of the Eucharist, but they are negligent, and do not use their ecclesiastical authority and power to effectively solve this problem. However, there are also many bishops who are unaware of the desecration of the Eucharist in their own dioceses and even in their own seminaries, because they never challenge their priests. Lack of communication and information can be sometimes astonishing, as it can be proven from the history of the Church. It is absolutely shocking what happened to the Armenians who did not accept the decrees of the Ecumenical Council of Chalcedon, which took place in 451, because they were misinformed that the Council of Chalcedon and Pope Leo I had allegedly followed the heresy of Nestorius. However, when they arrived at the Ecumenical Council of Florence, they realized that this was totally false. In the *Bull of union with the Armenians* of the said Council of Florence, formulated at Session 8, held on November 22, 1439, we read as follows: "Apart from the three Synods of Nicaea (325), Constantinople (381) and the first of Ephesus (431), the Armenians have accepted no other later universal synods nor the most blessed Leo, Bishop of this Holy See, by whose authority the Council of Chalcedon met. For they claim that it was proposed to them that both the Synod of Chalcedon and the said Leo had made the definition in accordance with the condemned heresy of Nestorius. So, we instructed them and declared that such a suggestion was false and that the Synod of Chalcedon and blessed Leo holily and rightly defined the truth of two natures in the one Person of Christ, described above, against the impious tenets of Nestorius and Eutyches. We commanded that for the future they should hold and venerate the most blessed Leo, who was a veritable pillar of the faith and replete with all sanctity and doctrine, as a saint deservedly inscribed in the calendar of the saints; and that they should reverence and respect, like the rest of the faithful, not only the three above-mentioned synods, but also all other universal synods legitimately celebrated by the authority of the Roman Pontiff."[80]

It is hard to believe that such a miscommunication and misinformation was possible in the Church, but it really took place. We can see how this lack of communication and information caused a division between the Armenians and the Apostolic See for centuries, for almost a 1000 years! In a very similar way, the Church is suffering today due to the profanation of the Eucharist, because many bishops do not check on the pastors who are in charge of the liturgical life in their dioceses, nor on those who are in charge of the priestly formation at their seminaries. However, blind trust can eviscerate and lay waste the field of the Church, and kill the faith and the spiritual life of many Catholics.

As it has been said in *FOREWORD*, the profanation of the Eucharist in the bosom of the Roman-Catholic Church in North America has been going on for approximately half a century! Priests are being appointed by Jesus Christ to "[minister] streams of clear teaching to the People of God."[81] Instead, many liberal, unfaithful and rebellious priests have infiltrated the minds and hearts of very many Catholics with their blurred, clouded, opaque teaching, leading them astray when they have released streams of the red rivers of the Innocent and Most Holy Blood of our LORD Jesus Christ which today are steadily flowing down through the thousands of sacrariums into the ground in so many places of North America. This demonic activity can be called – "Eucharistic abortion." As the Book of Revelation relates, the Heavenly City of Jerusalem is full of Divine Life which is depicted as "a pure river of water of life, clear as crystal, pro-

---

[80] N. P. Tanner, *vol. I*, op. cit., pp. 539–540.

[81] *The Roman Missal, Entrance Antiphon for the Memorial of Saint Bernard, Abbot and Doctor of the Church*, op. cit., p. 787.

ceeding from the throne of God and of the Lamb" (Revelation 22:1), and flowing down in the middle of the street of the city (cf. Revelation 22:2a). The pilgrim Church, on earth, already possesses this Divine Life, especially in the Blessed Sacrament of Holy Communion. There is nothing in the Church that is more precious than the Sacrament of the Living and Life-giving Body and Blood of Jesus Christ, the Son of the Living God. This Heavenly Gift, perpetually coming down to us from the throne of God and of the Lamb in the Eucharist, must be received and cherished by all of us on our knees with the most profound worship, faith and love, and never be so brutally wasted as it is today; this Heavenly Gift is to be accepted and remain in our hearts, not in the ground, because in the Sacrament of Holy Communion God communicates with His people, not with the ground; the Most Holy Communion expresses the most intimate and interpersonal communion between God and His people, and not an impersonal relation between God and the soulless soil.

Years ago the sacrariums were used very rarely, while the confessionals were full of penitents; today, the confessionals are empty, and in some churches are even difficult to be found, while the sacrariums are full of the Blood of Christ. This is a consequence of disobedience in the Roman-Catholic Church and of a lost sense of sin which can be traced back to the tragic moment when liberal bishops, priests and theologians openly rejected the Encyclical Letter *Humanae Vitae* of His Holiness Paul VI, promulgated on July 25, 1968. This *great* and *collective* disobedience of the liberal local leaders of the Roman-Catholic Church, who despised the Authority of the Holy Father (cf. 2 Peter 2:10a), has triggered an avalanche of disobedience among the clergy and the laity in North America. Through this *massive* and *collective* disobedience, expressed by the local ecclesiastical authorities, the clergy and the laity in North America have joined in the culture of death. Therefore, God charges those responsible for leadership in His Church with the profanation of the Eucharist, saying: "Those who guide this people are leading them astray, and those who are guided by them are brought to confusion" (Isaiah 9:15). "And those who handle the law did not know Me; the shepherds rebelled against Me" (Jeremiah 2:8b.c). "The prophets prophesy falsely, and the priests rule by their own power; and My people love to have it so. But what will you do in the end?" (Jeremiah 5:31).

The Encyclical *Humanae Vitae* is about man's respect for God, the Creator, and about the dignity and protection of human life. However, once the rebels laid violent hands on human life, evil began its course, and it was just a matter of time, when they also laid violent hands on God, the Author of Life, who is *truly*, *really* and *substantially* present in the Most Holy Eucharist. The words of the first and the second discourse of Saint Peter the Apostle echo here who says in the Acts of the Apostle: "Jesus of Nazareth, a Man attested by God to you by miracles, wonders, and signs which God did through Him in your midst, as you yourselves also know, Him, being delivered by the determined purpose and foreknowledge of God, you have taken by lawless hands, have crucified, and put to death" (Acts 2:22b–23); "you denied the Holy One and the Just [...], and killed the Prince of Life ..." (Acts 3:14–15). And without our Prince of Life, there is only a spiritual desolation. At the time of the Old Testament, God said to His rebellious people through the Prophet Micah: "I will [...] make you sick by striking you, by making you desolate because of your sins. You shall sow, but not reap; you shall tread olives, but not anoint yourselves with oil; you shall tread grapes, but not drink wine. You shall eat, but not be satisfied; hunger shall be in your midst" (Micah 6:13.15.14a.b; cf. Deuteronomy 28:38–40; Amos 5:11b; Haggai 1:6a.b.c).

The above-quoted texts can be understood in spiritual terms. When we look back on the last 50 years during which the Most Holy Eucharist has been profaned in North America, then we can imagine how many Catholics have been struck and made sick and desolate because of the sin of excommunication. Very many priests carried much seed to the field of the Church, but gathered little in, for the locust of the sin of excommunication consumed it (cf. Deuteronomy 28:38), leaving behind a spiritual desert, because they did not sow the seed of truth, but of error. They planted pleasant vineyards and tended them, but they neither drank the wine from them nor gathered the grapes, for the worm of disobedience to the liturgical regulations devoured them (cf. Deuteronomy 28:39; Amos 5:11b). They eat, but they are not satisfied, and they suffer spiritual hunger (cf. Micah 6:14a.b), since the spiritual hunger can be satisfied only by a spiritual food, and the spiritual food is the attitude of obedience to the will of God, as our LORD Jesus Christ teaches us, when He says: "My food is to do the will of Him who sent Me, and to finish His work" (John 4:34b). "[They] clothe [themselves], but no one is warm" (Haggai 1:6d), for they should be "clothed with righteousness" (Psalm 132:9) and "with salvation" (2 Chronicles 6:41b; Psalm 132:16); instead they are covered with the sin of excommunication and damnation. Although they were surrounded with the olive trees of God's Grace, they were not anointed with their oil, for their olives dropped off, when they did not attend to the voice of God speaking through His Holy Church (cf. Deuteronomy 28:40). Those who should be rich in God's graces "are wretched, miserable, poor, blind, and naked" (Revelation 3:17), "and he who earns wages, earns wages to put into a bag with holes" (Haggai 1:6e), in accordance with the words of our LORD who has said: "He who is not with Me is against Me, and he who does not gather with Me scatters" (Matthew 12:30). This, in turn, brings a spiritual desolation which so visibly and tangibly results in more and more abandoned churches, being closed one after another.

Although many new houses of worship have been built in the last five decades in North America, yet more and more of them are being closed or sold or demolished, for they are yawning with emptiness. Why? Because every house of God must be a dwelling place of the Holy Spirit. Where, however, the rebellious spirit of disobedience reigns, there the Spirit of God is not present. Here, the words of God, uttered through the Prophet Amos, resound who has said: "Though you have built houses of hewn stone, yet you shall not dwell in them" (Amos 5:11a). And the Prophet Micah prophesied: "Yet the land shall be desolate because of those who dwell in it, and for the fruit of their deeds" (Micah 7:13). This prophecy can be seen fulfilled in our days. There are many places where Roman-Catholic temples are empty because of the irresponsible attitude of their pastors, and because of their deeds. The disobedience and insanity of liberal priests have *internally* laid desolate the Roman-Catholic Church in North America, and the only One who can cure today's Church is God Himself about whom the Psalmist writes: "He turns a wilderness into pools of water, and dry land into water-springs. There He makes the hungry dwell, that they may establish a city for a dwelling place, and sow fields and plant vineyards, that they may yield a fruitful harvest" (Psalm 107:35–37).

The sacrilegious practice of pouring the Most Precious Eucharistic Blood of Christ into the sacrarium has been introduced by many unlearned priests who have totally ignored the law of the Church, acting by their own whim. All those who have contrived this insane, abortive and satanic practice have incurred an *automatic excommunication* reserved to the Apostolic See in accordance with what has been written in Canon 1367 of the *Code of Canon Law*:

> "A person who throws away the consecrated species or who takes them or retains them for a sacrilegious purpose incurs an *automatic (latae sententiae)* excommunication reserved to the Apostolic See; if a cleric, he can be punished with another penalty including dismissal from the clerical state."[82]

This juridical regulation of the Roman-Catholic Church has strongly been confirmed and reinforced by the afore-mentioned official Apostolic document, entitled: "Instruction on the Eucharist *Redemptionis Sacramentum*: On Certain Matters to Be Observed or to Be Avoided Regarding the Most Holy Eucharist," issued by the Congregation for Divine Worship and the Discipline of the Sacraments on March 25, 2004. Paragraph 107 of this document reads as follows:

> "In accordance with what is laid down by the canons: 'One who throws away the consecrated species or takes them away or keeps them for a sacrilegious purpose, incurs a *latae sententiae* excommunication reserved to the Apostolic See; a cleric, moreover, may be punished by another penalty, not excluding dismissal from the clerical

---

[82] *Code of Canon Law*, op. cit., p. 495.

state' [Code of Canon Law, can. 1367]. To be regarded as pertaining to this case is any action that is voluntarily and gravely disrespectful of the sacred species. Anyone, therefore, who acts contrary to these norms, for example, casting the sacred species into the sacrarium or in an unworthy place or on the ground, incurs the penalties laid down. Furthermore, all will remember that once the distribution of Holy Communion during the celebration of Mass has been completed, the prescriptions of the Roman Missal are to be observed, and in particular, whatever may remain of the Blood of Christ must be entirely and immediately consumed by the Priest or by another minister, according to the norms, while the consecrated hosts that are left are to be consumed by the Priest at the altar or carried to the place for the reservation of the Eucharist."[83]

The above-quoted Paragraph 107 of the liturgical instruction *Redemptionis Sacramentum*, regarding the casting of the sacred species into the sacrarium or in an unworthy place or on the ground, is absolutely clear and unequivocal; it clarifies without a shadow of a doubt that the practice of pouring the Most Holy Blood of our Savior into the sacrarium is totally wrong, as a most grave abuse, and that consequently this practice ensures the most serious ecclesiastical penalty which is – *excommunication*.

It is also noteworthy to call our attention to a very important document, entitled: "This Holy and Living Sacrifice: Directory for the Celebration and Reception of Communion under Both Kinds," formulated earlier by

---

[83] Instruction on the Eucharist *Redemptionis Sacramentum*, op. cit., pp. 49–50.

the Episcopal Conference of the United States on November 1, 1984. In Norm 38 of this document, it is stated the following:

> "It is strictly prohibited to pour the Precious Blood into the ground or into the sacrarium."[84]

The Bishops of the United States themselves instruct Catholics – following the law of the Church – that "it is strictly prohibited to pour the Precious Blood into the ground or into the sacrarium."

Finally, the earlier-quoted document: *Norms for the Distribution and Reception of Holy Communion Under Both Kinds in the Dioceses of the United States of America*, which is also printed in the *Roman Missal*, instructs in Norm 55 as follows:

> "The reverence due to the Precious Blood of the LORD demands that it be fully consumed after Communion is completed and never be poured into the ground or the sacrarium."[85]

The above-adduced Norm 55 is absolutely clear, namely, that the remaining Blood of Christ must be "fully consumed," after the distribution of the Eucharist is completed, and "never be poured into the ground or the sacrarium." What else needs to be said by the Roman-Catholic Church on this issue?

---

[84] *This Holy and Living Sacrifice: Directory for the Celebration and Reception of Communion under Both Kinds* (Washington, D.C. 1985), p. 17.

[85] *The Roman Missal*, op. cit., p. 85*.

The *Roman Missal* does not say anything about the moral and juridical consequences which the pouring of the Most Holy Blood of Christ into the ground or the sacrarium entails, because the purpose of the norms contained in the *Roman Missal* is to instruct Catholics on how the Eucharist is to be properly celebrated, not to inform about penalties which are incurred by those who do pour the Most Precious Blood of Christ into the ground or into the sacrarium; these penalties are detailed in the afore-said *Canon Law* and in the Instruction *Redemptionis Sacramentum*. The point is that the ground and/ or the sacrarium are NOT tabernacles. Let us NOT bury our LORD again! The celebration of the Eucharist is entrusted to the clergy who are to cherish it according to the ordinances of the Church, and all the regulations of the Church, pertaining to this Most Holy Sacrament, must never be consigned to oblivion, since they are meant to prevent the Eucharist from being abused.

The profanation of the Most Holy Eucharist is not only a lapse from the law of the Church, but first and foremost, it is a lapse from the Collective Faith of the Church, and this is the very core of the problem. Jesus Christ says that "a good man out of the good treasure of his heart brings forth good; and an evil man out of the evil treasure of his heart brings forth evil. For out of the abundance of the heart his mouth speaks" (Luke 6:45). If the heart of a priest does not believe in the real presence of Jesus Christ in the Eucharist, he should not celebrate it.

Moreover, in some seminaries, as mentioned above, the seminarians were *officially* taught that pouring the left-over Blood of Christ into the sacrarium was allegedly the commonly acceptable practice of the Roman-Catholic Church. In this manner, the profanation of the Eucharist was *falsely legitimized* and *authorized* by the false teachers and superiors of those seminaries. The Wisdom of God says on the pages of Sacred Scripture: "Honor and dishonor come from speaking, and the tongue of mortals may be their downfall" (Sirach 5:13). This statement is a perfect Biblical comment on all those pseudo-professors whose deceitful tongues led them, and those who followed them, to their spiritual downfall. I know of at least four seminaries, where the profanation of the Most Precious Blood of Christ took place, and I personally talked with seminarians and priests who testified that they were *officially* taught at their seminaries to pour the Most Holy Blood of Christ into the sacrarium. We can only imagine what kind of "priestly" formation was being given to the seminarians of those seminaries.

As Pope Leo X has said during the Fifth Lateran Council, at Session 8, held on December 19, 1513, "it does not suffice occasionally to clip the roots of the brambles, if the ground is not dug deeply so as to check them beginning again to multiply, and if there are not removed their seeds and root causes from which they grow so easily."[86] The very seeds and root causes from which the profanation of the Eucharist has grown, has been the disastrously low level of education at some seminaries.

On one occasion, a priest, who has been teaching at a seminary for over 20 years, invited me to dinner at a restaurant. We were engaged in a discussion, and in the course of our conversation, I broached the theme of the profanation of the Eucharist, as well as the problem that the seminarians are being wrongly instructed to pour the remaining Blood of Christ into the sacrarium. The priest immediately understood what I said, and, with a cynical smile on his face, he responded ironically: "Do you want to change the whole clergy in America?" "The American priests don't follow the law of the Church." I replied: "Father, there is no reason to smile. The

---

[86] N. P. Tanner, *vol. I*, op. cit., p. 606.

profanation of the Eucharist is a serious issue!" Having heard my strong-minded and unhesitating response, the priest became disconcerted. I went on, saying: "Canon Law and the Instruction *Redemptionis Sacramentum* are in force, and all the priests are obliged to follow the liturgical regulations of the Church." In turn, he answered: "The priests in America don't care for the law of the Church." This means that they ignore the Authorities of the Roman-Catholic Church who stand behind the ecclesiastical law. However, as Saint Ignatius of Antioch teaches, whoever acts apart from the Authorities of the Church "is not pure in his conscience,"[87] but he is a man with a seared conscience (cf. 1 Timothy 4:2). Consequently, he is prone to error. Then, trying to make a better picture of himself, the priest said: "I inform the seminarians privately how to act properly." What a coward! This poor priest does not have the courage to challenge the rector and the other teachers at his seminary, but he teaches the seminarians and the young priests "secretly." What good is it to them? When the seminarians and/ or the newly ordained priests are sent to the parishes, there they see the profanation of the Eucharist, lawlessly permitted by so many pastors, and they have no power to stop this terrible abuse, being often intimidated by their liberal pastors. This is a vicious circle. Trying to avoid being labeled as "troublemakers" or "disturbers" (cf. 1 Kings 21:20b), most of the seminarians and the young priests have given up, "for they loved the glory of men more than the Glory of God" (John 12:43). As a matter of fact, they become accomplices of the profanation of the Eucharist. They, indeed, could effectively contribute to ending the profanation of the Eucharist by a firm and courageous attitude, but they prefer to appease people rather than

---

[87] "From the beginning of a letter to the Trallians by Saint Ignatius of Antioch, bishop and martyr," in *The Liturgy of the Hours, vol. IV* (New York 1975), p. 352.

God. Many of them keep saying that they obey their pastors, and that's how under the cover of falsely perceived obedience the profanation of the Eucharist is being continued. So, a "private" and "secret" instruction by this poor afore-mentioned priest, pertaining to the profanation of the Eucharist, is to no avail. Right teaching must be implemented, otherwise it is only pure theory. The Eucharist is no secret in the Church, and it is to be taught openly, not – clandestinely.

All of those who profane the Eucharist are the false shepherds of the deceived and empty minds who themselves first need to return to the path of right and truth (cf. Pope Leo X at Session 11 of the Fifth Lateran Council held on December 19, 1516),[88] provided they want to guide the People of God. But unfortunately, too many of those who were appointed in the Church as teachers and superiors of the seminarians proved themselves to be blind leaders (cf. Matthew 15:14b; 23:16a.24), "and if the blind leads the blind, both will fall into a ditch" (Matthew 15:14c; cf. Luke 6:39). Jesus Christ is stern with those who blindly lead the People of God, when He says: "Woe to you, blind guides" (Matthew 23:16a), and protecting His people from blind guides, He gives them the following order: "Leave them alone. They are blind leaders of the blind" (Matthew 15:14a.b). This ditch into which fall those who profane the Most Sacred Blood of Jesus Christ is technically called – *excommunication*, and from this ditch they can be pulled out by their repentance and an absolution reserved to the Apostolic See. At this point, once again, I want to remind those who profane the Most Holy Eucharist that the penalties laid down by Canon Law and the Instruction *Redemptionis Sacramentum* are not a kind of juridical scarecrow. Since the profanation of the Most Precious Blood of Jesus Christ is a

---

[88] Cf. N. P. Tanner, *vol. I*, op. cit., p. 635.

crime committed against our Eucharistic LORD, it brings about very, very serious disciplinary ecclesiastical consequences on those who commit this disgraceful offence; the desecration of the Eucharist entails spiritual death, because that's what the *excommunication* is all about in its very nature.

Although the documents of the Roman-Catholic Church are very strong and unequivocal on this matter, many pastors profane the Most Precious Blood of Christ with impunity and, if that were not enough, they also command those who work with them, that is, the associate pastors, the deacons and the extraordinary Eucharistic ministers, to go along with them in this evil, demonic practice. The Apostle Paul writes to Timothy that "the sins of some people are clearly evident, preceding them to judgment, while the sins of others follow later" (1 Timothy 5:24). These words fit so perfectly all those pastors who with a full awareness profane the Eucharist and all those who blindly follow them. What is very sad and tragic is the fact that many pastors who profane the Eucharist, and teach others to do the same, even when they learn that pouring the Blood of Christ into the sacrarium is strictly prohibited in the Church, they do not show any contrition for their wrong doing, and they deliberately continue this evil practice, because they are those whom the Bible calls: "stiff-necked" (cf. Exodus 32:9b; 33:3b; 34:9b). They are those who "loved darkness rather than light, because their deeds were evil" (John 3:19); their sins are flagrant beyond any doubt, and they cry out for God's judgment. Truly they are stiff-necked priests comparable to those to whom God, in the past, sent the Prophet Ezekiel, saying: "Son of man, I am sending you to the Israelites, to a nation of rebels who have rebelled against Me; they and their ancestors have revolted against Me to this very day. They are hard of face and obstinate of heart. I am sending you to them, and you shall say to them, 'Thus says the LORD God.' As for them, whether they hear or whether they refuse – for they are a rebellious house – yet they will know that a prophet has been among them" (Ezekiel 2:3b–5). Those to whom God sent the Prophet Ezekiel were impudent and stubborn people. Defiance and intractability are their necklaces; their minds, hearts and souls are poisoned and consumed with their rebellious venom. They are spiritual wrecks who spiritually wreck many Catholics for whom our LORD has poured out His own Blood. Priests are to reflect in their service the Grace of God; instead, those priests who profane the Eucharist are clothed "with *dis*-grace" (Psalm 132:18); they are clothed with the shame of excommunication, as well as with the shame of misleading so many lay people, because they "have forsaken the fountain of wisdom" (Baruch 3:12), and they "seek falsehood" (Psalm 4:3b). All those who conscientiously and willfully profane the Most Holy Blood of Christ must carefully attend to the words of warning which Moses addressed to the Israelites, saying: "Let there be among you no root which bears poison or wormwood. If, after hearing this imprecation, anyone, blessing himself, should say in his heart, 'I shall have peace, even though I follow the dictates of my heart' [...], the LORD will not spare him; for then the wrath of the LORD and His jealousy will burn against that man, and every curse that is written in this book will fall on him, and the LORD will blot out his name from under heaven" (Deuteronomy 29:17b–19). And the Author of the Letter to the Hebrews writes: "See to it that no one misses the Grace of God, lest any root of bitterness springing up cause trouble, and by this many become defiled" (Hebrews 12:15). How accurate is this warning and how it fits the evil practice of the profanation of the Eucharist. Indeed, those who desecrated the Most Precious Blood of Christ missed the Grace of God; by their satanic defiance and disobedience to the official and authoritative teaching of the Roman-Catholic Church, they caused a very bitter root to spring up through which many became defiled. Those priests who profaned the Most Holy Blood of Christ, and forced others to follow them, were called to bring the faithful to Jesus Christ, this graceful and fruitful shoot that has sprung from the stem of Jesse and grown out of his roots (cf. Isaiah 11:1); they were morally obliged to constantly engraft the faithful into Jesus Christ, "the Branch of the LORD [...] beautiful and glorious" (Isaiah 4:2a); instead, they have cut them off from this Divine and Life-giving Branch and engrafted them into the branch which has sprung from the stump of the devil and grown out of his bitter and lifeless roots of death.

Already in the Early Church, there were many insubordinate, intractable and rebellious talkers and deceivers (cf. Titus 1:10). And today, all those priests who profane the Most Holy Communion, in the bosom of the Roman-Catholic Church, are our "false brothers" (Galatians 2:4) who mentally abuse and enslave the deacons and the extraordinary Eucharistic ministers by teaching and commanding them to pour the Most Precious Blood of Christ into the sacrarium. Being entitled to lead the People of God, they *mis*-lead them and make them the slaves of their insane and sacrilegious practice. Our LORD says that "whoever commits sin is a slave of sin" (John 8:34b). As mentioned above, the sin of the profanation of the Eucharist is so great that it entails the sentence of excommunication, and everyone who is excommunicated is out of the Church. Thus, the slavery to this sin brings about a separation from Jesus Christ Himself, because he who is separated from the Mystical Body of the Church is simultaneously separated from the LORD who is the Head of His Holy Church (cf. Colossians 1:18a). One day, Moses said about the Israelites who basely treated their God: "They have corrupted themselves; they are not His children, because of their blemish: A perverse and crooked generation. Do you thus repay the LORD, O foolish and senseless people? Is He not your Father, who created you? Has He not made you and established you?" (Deuteronomy 32:5–6). And through the Prophet Jeremiah God also warned the shepherds of Israel, saying: "Woe to the shepherds who destroy and scatter the sheep of My pasture! [...] You have scattered My flock, driven them away, and not attended to them. Behold, I will attend to you for the evil of your doings ..." (Jeremiah 23:1–2).

At this point, one could raise a question: Why do so many priests not want to stop the profanation of the Eucharist even when they know that it is strictly prohibited to pour the Most Holy Blood of Christ into the sacrarium under pain of excommunication? The answer is very simple. They are ashamed and have no courage to admit that they have so wrongly instructed the deacons and extraordinary Eucharistic ministers pertaining to what they should do with the remaining Blood of Christ. But it is better to be ashamed now than to be condemned for eternity on the Day of the Last Judgment. It is beyond any doubt that it is their demonic pride that treads them down. Their disgraceful pride is the greatest obstacle which they must overcome if they want to re-establish their full communion with Jesus Christ and His Holy Church, but unfortunately many of them prefer to keep the profanation of the Eucharist going on than to admit their tragic mistake, and along with their rebellious attitude they drag down the People of God. Seeing this, God complains today, just as He had in the past at the time of the Prophet Isaiah, saying: "O My people, those who guide you lead you astray, and confuse the course of your paths" (Isaiah 3:12b). Because those who were responsible for the spiritual leadership in the Church failed; therefore, God announces that He Himself will guide His people, when He says through the Prophet Isaiah: "I will bring the blind by a way they did not know; I will lead them in paths they have not known. I will make darkness light before them, and crooked places straight. These things I will do for them, and not forsake them" (Isaiah 42:16). Indeed, God will make darkness light and crooked places straight when finally the profanation of the Most Holy Eucharist in the Roman-Catholic Church in North America will completely cease, and God can achieve it even through the laity.

I know a parish where the extraordinary Eucharistic ministers were wrongly instructed to pour the Most Precious Blood of Christ into the sacrarium. But one day, they were informed by a man that this practice was strictly prohibited in the Roman-Catholic Church. Immediately they challenged their pastor by presenting to him Norm 38 of the *Directory for the Celebration and Reception of Communion under Both Kinds* written by the Episcopal Conference of the United States on November 1, 1984. However, the pastor, in his arrogance, said to them: "I will not change anything." Thereupon, the extraordinary Eucharistic ministers responded: "But we will never again pour the Blood of Christ into the sacrarium." This case is a classical example of a diabolically evil and false shepherd. Unfortunately there are many priests like him throughout North America. Instead of keeping watch over themselves and over all the flock of Jesus Christ, of which the Holy Spirit has made them overseers, to shepherd the Church of God that He has obtained with the Blood of His own Son (cf. Acts 20:28), the priests who profane the Most Holy Eucharist act as savage wolves that do not spare the flock of the LORD (cf. Acts 20:29); they have been called by God to gather the faithful people together in Jesus Christ (cf. Matthew 23:37; Luke 13:34), but in effect, they act as soulless and corrupt hirelings who scatter the sheep of the LORD (cf. John 10:12).

All these priests in question also scandalize the little ones, as for instance, the altar-boys and altar-girls, who come to serve at Holy Mass, and whose faith in the real presence of Jesus Christ in the Most Holy Eucharist is gradually being killed, this precious faith which their parents and teachers have aroused and formed in them. Of these priests, who commit this crime, the words of our LORD are true: "It is impossible that no offenses should come, but woe to him through whom they do come! It would be better for him if a millstone were hung around his neck, and he were thrown into the sea, than that he should offend one of these little ones" (Luke 17:1–2; cf. Matthew 18:6; Mark 9:42).

One day a woman told me how she was terrified by what she had heard from her son who was serving in her parish as an altar-boy. He confided to her that he had personally seen how the Most Precious Blood of Christ had been poured into the sacrarium by the extraordinary Eucharistic ministers in the sacristy of the church. She was very much perplexed and concerned not only about the very fact of the profanation of the Eucharist, but about the faith and the spiritual life of her son as well. Having heard this I said to her: "Please, don't allow your son to continue to serve in your parish as an altar-boy, otherwise he will completely lose his faith in the real presence of Jesus Christ in the Eucharist." Then I heard her say: "Thank you, Father, for what you have just said; I myself was thinking about the same." I also encouraged her to talk to the parents whose children were serving in her parish as altar-boys and altar-girls to persuade them to join her in her effort to prevent their children from seeing this terrible and damnable abuse of the Eucharist.

However, sometimes the defiance of lay people can also be no less satanic than that of evil priests who profane the Eucharist. I personally know two priests from a diocese who were assigned together to the same parish at the same time. As soon as they began their priestly service in their new parish, they became aware of the profanation of the Eucharist. Both of them strongly reacted against this practice, instructing the extraordinary Eucharistic ministers that the Blood of Christ must be completely consumed and never poured into the sacrarium, but they did not want to obey their instruction. So, these pious priests decided that one of them will always be present in the sacristy at the time when the extraordinary Eucharistic ministers were bringing the remaining Blood of Christ after the distribution of Holy Communion during Holy Mass. These faithful priests simply blocked the way to the sacrarium with their bodies, not permitting the extraordinary Eucharistic ministers to pour the Precious Blood of Christ into the sacrarium. The ministers reacted with anger, and some of them, while shaking their fists at the noses of the priests, cried out: "We will show you that you will be kicked out of our parish." Weekend by weekend, these loyal priests were oppressed by the rebellious conduct of the wicked (cf. 2 Peter 2:7). Ironically, this incident took place in a diocese whose ordinary was universally known and esteemed as a solid and orthodox bishop, and later he was even promoted and elevated to a higher position in the Roman-Catholic Church.

A similar story took place in another diocese where one of my classmates served in a parish as an associate pastor. He fervently asked his pastor to stop the pouring of the Blood of Christ into the sacrarium, but in vain. Because he did not receive any support from his corrupt pastor, he decided to solve the problem by himself. First, he talked with the extraordinary Eucharistic ministers, trying to induce them to stop this evil practice, but they, like his pastor, ignored him. Then this faithful priest decided to take everything in his own hands, and he acted similarly as the above-mentioned two priests; every weekend, at the time when he did not celebrate Holy Mass, he waited Mass after Mass, in the sacristy, for the extraordinary Eucharistic ministers, and when they brought in the chalices with the remaining Blood of Christ, with the intention of pouring it into the sacrarium, he took the chalices from them and he himself consumed the Blood of Christ. He did this for two years; then he left the parish.

The above-adduced stories show how the faith in the real presence of our LORD Jesus Christ in the Eucharist must be renewed among lay people. I know a monk who served as a visiting priest in the parish of a very large city on weekends. One Sunday he came to the sacristy of the church and asked the sacristan for the key to the tabernacle to check the number of available Holy Hosts. To his great surprise the sacristan said to him: "I have already checked; there were not many Hosts, but I added more." This incident proves beyond any doubt that this poor man did not know at all what the Most Holy Communion is about. For him the Eucharist was just a piece of bread and nothing else. But we should not be surprised: How can we expect faith in the Most Holy Eucharist from lay people when so many priests themselves do not believe in it, and even profane it?

Julian Herranz writes in his commentary on "Safeguarding the Bread of Life Come down From Heaven," enclosed in Volume XIV of *The Canon Law Digest*, as follows:

> "Therefore we can understand the care and efforts of the Church's Pastors to see that this priceless Gift is deeply and devoutly loved, safeguarded and surrounded with that worship which expresses in the best way humanly possible

our faith in Christ's real presence – Body, Blood, Soul and Divinity – under the Eucharistic Species, even after the Holy Sacrifice has been celebrated.

Just as believers are asked to express this faith with actions, prayers and objects of noble dignity, so it is also advisable that any kind of carelessness or negligence, the sign of a diminished sense of the Eucharistic Divine presence, be carefully avoided in the behaviour of sacred ministers and the faithful. Indeed, in our age, marked by haste even in one's personal relationship with God, catechesis should reacquaint the Christian people with the whole of Eucharistic worship, which cannot be reduced to participation in Holy Mass and to receiving Communion with the proper dispositions, but also includes frequent adoration – personal and communal – of the Blessed Sacrament, and the loving concern that the tabernacle – in which the Eucharist is kept – be placed on an altar or in a part of the church that is clearly visible, truly noble and duly adorned, so that it is a center of attraction for every heart in love with Christ.

In contrast to such profound veneration for the true Bread come down from heaven, not only can deplorable disciplinary abuses occur, sometimes have occurred and still occur, but even acts of contempt and profanation on the part of individuals who, under almost diabolical inspiration, dare to oppose in this way whatever the Church and the faithful hold, adore and love as Most Sacred.

> In order to deter those who let themselves be misled by such sentiments, the Church not only urges the faithful to avoid any form of disgraceful carelessness and negligence, but also considers the most unfortunate case of deliberate acts of hatred or contempt for the Blessed Sacrament. These actions certainly constitute – by reason of their matter – a very grave sin of sacrilege."[89]

On the one hand, the author of the above-quoted commentary reminds the reader of the Sacredness of the Sacrament of the Eucharistic Body and Blood of our LORD and, on the other hand, he recalls the "deplorable disciplinary abuses" of the Eucharist, the "acts of contempt and profanation on the part of individuals [...] under almost diabolical inspiration" and even "the most unfortunate case of deliberate acts of hatred or contempt for the Blessed Sacrament."

Julian Herranz is absolutely right in his observations. I personally met liberal priests who hated the exposition of the Blessed Sacrament and sneered at those who adored the Eucharistic Jesus. In the last few decades, there was no exposition of the Blessed Sacrament in many seminaries in North America where the superiors, who were responsible for priestly formation of the seminarians, falsely kept saying that the adoration of the Blessed Sacrament is theologically incorrect. A young priest told me that when he was in the seminary, he and his class-mates were requesting, for months, their rector and other superiors for exposition of the Blessed Sacrament. But their response was: "Who will do it?" It is hard to believe

---

[89] J. Herranz, "Safeguarding the Bread of Life Come down From Heaven," [in]: *The Canon Law Digest, vol. XIV* (ed. P. J. Cogan; Washington, D.C. 2012), pp. 1133–1134.

that no priest in that seminary wanted to expose the Blessed Sacrament to be adored by the seminarians. I myself know a large and influential seminary in North America from which the seminarians were *secretly* going to a chapel in a neighboring town where there was an exposition of the Blessed Sacrament, because they were afraid of being classified as fanatical and narrow-minded by their superiors who were very liberal, and who had little respect for Catholic piety. The situation at the seminary changed with the coming of the new bishop, but prior to his installation, those corrupt superiors did a lot of evil to many good seminarians whom they kicked out from the said seminary, because they did not want to follow their liberalism. However, some of those seminarians did not quit; they were accepted by other dioceses and were ordained to the priesthood. One of my dear friends, who was my best pastor, and who was graduated from the seminary in question, told me that one day he was invited by a newly ordained priest to his first Mass in his parish, followed by a reception. There were many priests present at the reception, and it happened that my friend was seated at the same table with *eight* priests who were removed from the above-mentioned seminary, but were ordained by bishops of other dioceses. Thanks be to God that these good men did not lose their faith, and did not say: "Good-bye" to their priestly vocation, but, through their perseverance, resisted the evil which their former superiors were sowing at the seminary, following diabolical inspiration.

"Since in our days (which we endure with sorrow) the sower of cockle, the ancient enemy of the human race (cf. Matthew 13:25.28), has dared to scatter and multiply in the LORD's field |this| extremely pernicious |abuse| (Pope Leo X at Session 8 of the Fifth Lateran Council held on December

19, 1513),"[90] which is the profanation of the Most Holy Eucharist, we must be more vigilant, lest the entire field of the LORD be sown with the cockle of this demonic practice, and the seed of faith be choked by the seed of evil (cf. Matthew 13:7; Mark 4:7; Luke 8:7). Saint Peter the Apostle warns us, writing: "Be sober and alert. Your enemy the devil prowls around like a roaring lion looking for someone to devour. Resist him, steadfast in your faith, knowing that the same sufferings are experienced by your brotherhood in the world" (1 Peter 5:8–9). Sacred Scripture says: "The wicked man does deceptive work, but he who sows righteousness will have a sure reward" (Proverbs 11:18). We must sow the seed of sound doctrine and of good education which will prevent the faithful from deadly errors. All of us Catholics are individually and collectively responsible for the spiritual welfare of the Church of Jesus Christ. "Like the Samaritan in the Gospel (cf. Luke 10:34), [we must undertake anew] the task of healing with oil and wine, lest that rebuke of Jeremiah may be cast at us: 'Is there no balm in Gilead, is there no physician there?' (Jeremiah 8:22a) (Pope Leo X at Session 8 of the Fifth Lateran Council held on December 19, 1513)."[91] "Why, then, is there no recovery for the health of the daughter of My people?" (Jeremiah 8:22b). Indeed, the Daughter Church in North America suffers greatly. "There is no health in [her] flesh [...], nor any health in [her] bones because of [her] sin. For [her] iniquities have gone over [her] head; like a heavy burden, they are too heavy for [her]. [Her] wounds are foul and festering because of [her] foolishness" (Psalm 38:4–6). Therefore, God says to her: "What shall I do with you [...]? For your love is like a morning cloud, and like the early dew which goes away. [...] For

---

[90] N. P. Tanner, *vol. I*, op. cit., p. 605.
[91] Ibid.

I desire love and not sacrifice, and the knowledge of God more than burnt offerings" (Hosea 6:4a.c.d.6; cf. Ecclesiastes 5:1; Matthew 9:13b; 12:7b). "Behold, to obey [God] is better than sacrifice ..." (1 Samuel 15:22c). And this is why the Blood of Christ is being profaned for so long a time. Because those who commit this terrible crime have no knowledge of God; they have no faith in the real presence of our LORD in Holy Communion; consequently, they have no love for the Eucharistic Jesus which, in turn, entails their disobedience, inasmuch as obedience to our LORD and to His Holy Church is a sign of love for Him and for His Church. Those who desecrate the Most Sacred Blood of the Incarnate Son of God are seriously wounded in their souls and are spiritually bleeding. However, Jesus Christ is our Heavenly Physician who will never drive away anyone who comes to Him (cf. John 6:37), for He is "meek and humble of heart" (Matthew 11:29). He pours forth in abundance the oil of His redemptive alleviation; He lavishes the balm of His salvific Mercy and He heals with the Wine of His Divine Love (cf. Luke 10:34), but those who are sick spiritually (cf. Matthew 9:12b; Mark 2:17b; Luke 5:31b) must turn to Him with a humbled spirit and a contrite heart (cf. Psalm 51:19).

The desecration of the Eucharist in the Roman-Catholic Church in North America could significantly be lessened by the faithful attitude of the priests who come from abroad, but tragically, many priests who come to North America from foreign countries succumb to the sin of the profanation of the Eucharist, although they know that pouring the Blood of Christ into the sacrarium is strictly prohibited in the Roman-Catholic Church. They do it, because they are intimidated by the local clergy, and they have neither faith nor courage to resist this evil practice. They slavishly get along with the local pastors, although not in their hearts, but only out of fear of being removed from their parishes. The truth is that they prefer to profane the Eucharist than to lose their pay-checks. "For all seek their own interests, not those of Jesus Christ" (Philippians 2:21). If they really loved Him, they would not seek their own (cf. 1 Corinthians 13:5), but as it truly is, they love the "mighty" dollar more than the Almighty God. I ask you, lovers of mammon: Where is your faith? The following words of the Bible so perfectly fit your cowardice and greed: "Blessed is every one who fears the LORD, who walks in His ways" (Psalm 128:1), but "cursed is the man who trusts in man and makes flesh his strength, whose heart departs from the LORD" (Jeremiah 17:5b). Your flesh "is overlaid with gold and silver, yet in it there is no breath at all" (Habakkuk 2:19c). Yes, your money-bag bulges, but your spirit shrinks; you gather mammon to feed your flesh, but your soul is starving. "Your riches are corrupted, and your garments are moth-eaten. Your gold and silver are corroded, and their corrosion will be a witness against you and will eat your flesh like fire" (James 5:2–3a). Now, listen to what the Wisdom of God has to say to you on the pages of Sacred Scripture: "Fear God and keep His commandments, for this is man's all" (Ecclesiastes 12:13b), and again: "Receive My instruction instead of silver, and knowledge rather than choice gold. For Wisdom is better than jewels, and all the things one may desire cannot be compared with Her" (Proverbs 8:10–11; cf. 3:15; Wisdom 7:8). Therefore, "if any of you lacks wisdom, let him ask of God, who gives to all liberally and without reproach, and it will be given to him" (James 1:5). If the instruction of Divine Wisdom is preferable to silver and Her knowledge to choice gold; if She is better than jewels, and all the things one may desire cannot be compared with Her, then how incomparably more Precious is the Priceless Blood of Jesus Christ who is the Son of the Living God and the Incarnate Wisdom of God. And the Wisdom of God says: "Riches and honor are with Me, enduring wealth and righteousness. My fruit is better than gold, yes, than pure gold, and My revenue than choice silver" (Proverbs 8:18–19; cf. 3:14.16). Therefore, "seek good and not evil, that you may live; so the LORD God of Hosts will be with you [...]. Hate evil, love good" (Amos 5:14–15a), and pray to God together with the Psalmist, saying: "Incline my heart to your decrees, and not to gain" (Psalm 119:36). "I will never forget your precepts, for by them you have given me life" (Psalm 119:93). "I have sworn and confirmed that I will observe your righteous ordinances" (Psalm 119:106). "Your decrees are my heritage forever; they are the joy of my heart. I incline my heart to perform your statutes forever, to the very end" (Psalm 119:111–112). What follows is opportunity for your profession of faith in the Eucharistic Jesus Christ. Our LORD says: "Do not lay up for yourselves treasures on earth, where moth and rust destroy and where thieves break in and steal; but lay up for yourselves treasures in heaven, where neither moth nor rust destroys and where thieves do not break in and steal. For where your treasure is, there your heart will be also" (Matthew 6:19–21; Luke 12:34). "Sell what you have and give alms; provide yourselves money bags which do not grow old, a treasure in the heavens that does not fail, where no thief approaches nor moth destroys" (Luke 12:33). But you, lovers of mammon, prefer the treasures of this passing world. Take to your heart the lesson of Saint James the Apostle who cries out: "Your gold and silver are corroded, and their corrosion will be a witness against you and will eat your flesh like fire" (James 5:3a). Change your mind and accept the exhortation of Saint Ignatius of Antioch who says: "Do not have Jesus Christ on your lips and the world in your hearts."[92] We, priests, are sent by Jesus Christ not to be bankers or tax-collectors, but shepherds of His People.

However, there are also some good priests who come from foreign countries to North America and strongly oppose the profanation of the Eucharist. I personally know a priest from South America who was sent to a parish, to serve as an associate pastor, where he almost immediately found the Most Holy Blood of Christ was being poured into the sacrarium. He informed his bishop about this liturgical abuse, but the bishop did not take any measures; however, under the pressure of his pastor, this righteous priest was removed from that parish after only two weeks of serving in it. The criminal was not punished, but the one who pointed out the criminal action, was. This blessed priest who defended the Eucharistic Jesus spoke later with his bishop about the problem of the profanation of the Eucharist, but the bishop responded, saying: "There is no profanation of the Eucharist in our diocese." The said priest also informed me that he had encouraged other priests from South America, who worked with him in that same diocese, that they should resist the profanation of the Most Precious Blood of Christ. But they said: "The bishop knows about the problem, and we have pledged our obedience to him." What a vicious circle! The irresponsible bishop does not want to investigate the problem of the profanation of the Eucharist, which takes place under his territorial Episcopal jurisdiction, claiming, despite the obvious facts, that there is no profanation of the Eucharist in his diocese, and the priests who are fully aware of this liturgical abuse do not want to challenge their bishop out of fear before him. They know that the pouring of the Most Holy Blood of our LORD into

---

[92] "From a letter to the Romans by Saint Ignatius of Antioch, bishop and martyr," in *The Liturgy of the Hours, vol. III* (New York 1975), p. 329.

the sacrarium is a deadly crime in the Church which incurs an excommunication, but they are not strong enough to act accordingly, because their faith has already been seriously weakened by their unfaithful bishop and pastors. Saint Augustine admonishes us that we are "to do nothing which might lead our weak brother into thinking evil of us. Otherwise, as we feed on the good pasture and drink the pure water, we may trample on God's meadow, and weaker sheep will have to feed on trampled grass and drink from troubled waters."[93] And that's what many wicked priests do to thousands of Catholics in North America today and even more; by their defiance and lack of faith, the corrupt priests not only cause the sheep of Christ "to feed on trampled grass and drink from troubled waters," but they also kill the sheep of Christ spiritually when they scandalize them by their own rebellious behavior and even try to encourage them to shed the Most Holy, the Most Precious and the Most Innocent Blood of our Divine LORD by pouring it into the sacrarium.

Some of the priests are so indifferent in their consciences that they do not care even for the Eucharistic particles of the Consecrated Bread that accidentally fall down on the ground. One of my friends, who came to North America from England, was assigned to a parish where he served as an associate pastor. One day, he found on the floor in his church an abandoned and crumbled Holy Host, probably trampled on by someone accidentally, and he began to pick up the particles from the floor in order to consume them. Thereupon, a priest came into the church and, seeing what my friend was doing, sneered at him, sarcastically saying: "O, here is a little Jesus and there is a little Jesus."

---

[93] "From a sermon by Saint Augustine, bishop," [in]: *The Liturgy of the Hours, vol. III* (New York 1975), p. 428.

I myself was at a parish where, one day, a pious woman found some fragments of the Consecrated Bread after Mass and she brought them to the pastor. He looked at her and said: "Whatever falls on the ground is not the Eucharist. Jesus always knows beforehand what will be consumed and what will not; therefore, all the particles of the Eucharist that happened to fall on the ground have never been consecrated." That's how many priests treat the left-over parts of the Eucharist. In a similar way, they treat the Consecrated Wine, saying: "Jesus always knows in advance how much Consecrated Wine will be drunk, and what remains is not the Eucharist, because it has, in fact, never been consecrated." There are also priests who say: "If Jesus knows how to 'jump into' bread and wine, He also knows how to 'jump out of' them." What insanity! This is the most arrogant and senseless comment on the Eucharist I have ever heard.

In the first place, those who contrived this absurd theory deny the teaching of the Catholic Church on *transubstantiation*. The Ecumenical Council of Trent, in the above-quoted Chapter 4 of the *Decree on the Most Holy Sacrament of the Eucharist* formulated at its Session 13, held on October 11, 1551, states that "by the consecration of the bread and wine, there takes place the change of the whole substance of the bread into the substance of the Body of our LORD Jesus Christ, and of the whole substance of the wine into the substance of His Blood. And the Holy Catholic Church has suitably and properly called this change transubstantiation."[94] The Consecrated Bread and the Consecrated Wine are not vessels in which our LORD dwells, since by the Words of Consecration the whole substance of the bread is changed into the substance of the Body of Christ, and the whole substance of the wine is changed into the substance of His

---

[94] N. P. Tanner, *vol. II*, op. cit., p. 695.

Blood. Consequently, there is no *con-substantiation* or *co-substance* in the Eucharist, that is to say, after the consecration, the substance of the bread and the substance of the wine do not co-exist with the Substance of the Body and Blood of Jesus Christ, but the whole substance of the bread and the whole substance of the wine change into the Substance of the Body and Blood of our LORD. The Consecrated Bread and the Consecrated Wine are Jesus Christ Himself, Living and Life-giving.

Secondly, the said Council of Trent, in its *Canons on the Most Holy Sacrament of the Eucharist*, given at the same Session 13, exhorts, in Canon 4, as follows:

> "If anyone says that the Body and Blood of our LORD Jesus Christ are not present in the wondrous Sacrament of the Eucharist after the completion of the consecration, but only in its use, while it is being consumed, but not before or after; and that the True Body of the LORD does not remain in the hosts or consecrated particles which are reserved or remain over after the Communion: let him be anathema."[95]

Consequently, those who say: "If Jesus knows how to 'jump into' bread and wine, He also knows how to 'jump out of' them" deny the official, authoritative and dogmatic teaching of the Catholic Church, and – according to the above-adduced Canon 4 – they are anathema, that is to say, they are excommunicated; they are outside the Church.

---

[95] Ibid., p. 697.

Thirdly, the terminology itself is highly disrespectful and offensive which can be used only by routinized, stupefied, soulless and paganized liturgical "robots." Whoever applies the expressions: "jump into" and/ or "jump out of" in reference to the Mystery of the Most Holy Eucharist has no sense of Sacredness concerning the sacrament which, as the only one of all seven sacraments, makes the *Divine Substance* present not only in the Church, but in the entire universe as well. The statements about our LORD "jumping into" and/ or "jumping out of" bread and wine can be classified only as imbecility. The intelligence of the one who uses such expressions can be compared to the intelligence of Rehoboam, one of the sons of Solomon about whom Sacred Scripture says that he was "expansive in folly, [and] limited in sense" (Sirach 47:23a). It was Rehoboam "who by his policy made the people rebel" (Sirach 47:23a; see also 1 Kings 12:2.20.26–32). Likewise, many priests today have made many Catholics rebels by the practice of the profanation of the Eucharist. Those who talk about Jesus who "jumps into" and/ or "out of" the Eucharist are not only the people with mindless heads, but also those who, by their perverse opinions, make others rebel in the Roman-Catholic Church. The Bible says: "The fool speaks foolishness, and his heart works iniquity, to practice ungodliness, to utter error against the LORD ..." (Isaiah 32:6a). And in another place: "A fool's explanation is like a burden on a journey ..." (Sirach 21:16). Yes, some heretical priests who have a wrong perception of the Eucharist simply talk rubbish. Some of their explanations pertaining to this Most Holy Sacrament are, indeed, like heavy bundles on a journey, and the more they senselessly carry them by the sweat of their brow the more they hunch their backs until their noses turn into ploughshares ploughing the soil which brings forth spiritual thorns and thistles to them (cf. Genesis 3:18). They only need to obey God and to follow the teaching of the Roman-Catholic Church. Then their heads will be lifted up, the sweat of their brow will be wiped out, and God Himself will cause their spiritual growth (cf. 1 Corinthians 3:7), "for He pours gifts on His beloved even while they slumber" (Psalm 127:2b). If only they obeyed the teaching of the Church, their priestly service would produce an abundance of good fruit, and the words of Jesus Christ would be fulfilled in their ministry who says in the Gospel: "Come to Me, all you who labor and are heavy laden, and I will give you rest. Take My yoke upon you and learn from Me, for I am gentle and humble in heart, and you will find rest for your souls. For My yoke is easy and My burden is light" (Matthew 11:28–30). Indeed, the yoke and burden of obedience and truth in the service of God are incomparably easier and lighter than the heavy bundles of defiance and error in the service of the devil. Those obstinate priests who profane the Eucharist are the victims of a fruitless drudgery which only brings forth cursed thorns and thistles of excommunication instead of the blessed fruits of Divine Grace and communion with the Church of Christ (cf. Genesis 3:17c–18). It is unimaginable that so many priests treat the Eucharistic Jesus so disrespectfully and brutally. Even their greatest pastoral efforts will not bring any good spiritual harvest unless the profanation of the Eucharist ceases. Thus, on them the words of the Prophet Haggai fulfill themselves who says: "Consider your ways! You have sown much, and bring in little" (Haggai 1:5b.6a). Why? Because they willfully flout the doctrine of the Roman-Catholic Church on the Eucharist and act contrary to it (cf. 1 Timothy 1:10), and being ignorant of how to direct their steps in the way of the Church, they persevere in their hardness of heart (cf. Pope Eugenius IV at Session 3 of the Council of Ferrara held on February 15, 1438).[96] The profanation of the Most Holy Eucharist has brought forth a lot of thorns and thistles (cf. Genesis 3:18) in the field of the Roman-Catholic Church. Therefore, using the language of the Ecumenical Council of Constance, we can say that the Church must act against those who profane the Eucharist "as against spurious and illegitimate sons, and to cut away their errors from the LORD's field as if they were harmful briars, by means of vigilant care and the knife of ecclesiastical authority, lest they spread as a cancer to destroy others (the Council of Constance, at Session 15, held on July 6, 1415)."[97]

All the priests who have profaned the Most Holy Eucharist have, by this very fact, *automatically* incurred "the penalty of *excommunication* from which, except at the imminent approach of death, they can be absolved *only* by the Roman Pontiff."[98] And since those irresponsible priests, who desecrated the Most Blessed Sacrament of the Eucharist, have incurred the *automatic* penalty of *excommunication*, by virtue of the ecclesial law itself, consequently, they also have *automatically* been *suspended*, by the said law, from exercising their orders. There were also many irresponsible people in the Early Church (cf. Titus 1:10) about whom the Apostle of the Nations writes that "they profess to know God, but they deny Him by their actions, being abominable, disobedient and disqualified for every good work" (Titus 1:16). Here, there can be seen a particular reference to all who profane the Most Holy Eucharist. Indeed, those who committed the horrific sin of the desecration of the Blood of Christ, by their disobedience to the faith and to the law of the Roman-Catholic Church, have been

---

[96] Cf. ibid., *vol. I*, pp. 518–519.
[97] Ibid., pp. 426–427.
[98] Ibid., p. 638.

"disqualified for every good work" in the Church by what they have taught about and done to the Eucharist. Those priests who personally poured the Most Holy Blood of Christ into the sacrarium and/ or taught others to do the same, have incurred an excommunication.

Now, those who are excommunicated, be it from among the clergy and/ or the laity, are outside the Church; consequently, they are unable to perform fruitful work in the bosom of the Church. They are deprived of their privilege to serve in the Roman-Catholic Church, because everyone who is *excommunicated* is *automatically* cut off from the Church. Moreover, in the case of priests who are excommunicated, they must NOT exercise their priestly ministry in the Church, that is to say, they must NOT celebrate Holy Mass, nor administer the other sacraments for this simple reason that they are out of the Church! As for lay people who knew about the liturgical regulations of the Roman-Catholic Church, which prohibit pouring the Most Holy Blood of Christ into the sacrarium, but still profaned the Most Holy Eucharist with full awareness, they also incurred an excommunication. Consequently, they must NOT receive the Eucharist so long as they did not receive an absolution from the Apostolic See. The Eucharist is reserved only for those who are in full communion with the Roman-Catholic Church, but those who are excommunicated have lost their full union with the Church. As one can see, the sin of the profanation of the Eucharist has ruined the spiritual life of our Mother Church, inasmuch as the moral and disciplinary consequences are unimaginably enormous and devastating not only for the abusers themselves of this Most Blessed Sacrament, but also for the whole Mystical Body of the Church, for the entire Community of the Faithful. Those corrupt priests – the profaners of the Most Holy Eucharist, swerving away from the straight ecclesiastical line into paths of satanic error (cf. the Council of Florence, at Session 7 held on September 4, 1439)[99] – have injected many other priests, deacons and extraordinary Eucharistic ministers with their poison of "sacrilegious arrogance" (The Council of Ferrara, at Session 3 held on February 15, 1438),[100] inclining them to perpetrate so scandalous, nefarious and detestable a crime. This tragic lapse has confused many Catholics, has severely damaged their faith in the real presence of Jesus Christ in the Eucharist and has led them nowhere due to the lack of true and faithful pastoral leadership. "Therefore, the people wander like sheep; they suffer for lack of a shepherd" (Zechariah 10:2c; cf. Numbers 27:17; Ezekiel 34:5a; Matthew 9:36).

Those priests who desecrate the Eucharist confuse the People of God and then leave them like sheep without a shepherd, because they themselves are confused intellectually and spiritually. On the one hand, they teach with their lips about the profundity of the Sacrament of the Most Holy Communion, how our LORD Jesus Christ is really present in the Eucharist and how precious this sacrament is, but on the other hand, by their sacrilegious practices, they contradict that which they preach, when they falsely instruct others to pour into the sacrarium the Blood of the One whom they acknowledge as their God and Savior, but only with their lips, not with their minds and hearts. By their deeds, they deny that which they teach. That is insanity! They forget that the pastoral service must always be in compliance with the doctrine of the Church. There must be an organic relationship and unity between *lex credendi* and *lex orandi*, that is, between *the law of belief* and *the law of worship*. What we believe is to be expressed in our worship, and what we worship is to be rooted in and come from our faith.

---

[99] Ibid., p. 531.
[100] Ibid., p. 519.

If we believe and teach that after the Words of Consecration the *whole* substance of the bread and the *whole* substance of the wine are *totally* changed into the Sacred Substance of the Eucharistic Jesus Christ, Body and Blood, Soul and Divinity, then consequently those who pour the Consecrated Wine into the sacrarium crucify our LORD over and over again.

Even at the time of the Old Testament, God complained about the shepherds of Israel in the following words: "The shepherds rebelled against Me" (Jeremiah 2:8d). "Many shepherds have ruined My vineyard; they have trodden My portion underfoot; they have made My pleasant portion a desolate wilderness" (Jeremiah 12:10). How beautifully God calls the People of Israel – "My pleasant portion." However, many false shepherds made this chosen heritage of God YHWH "a desolate wilderness." That's exactly what evil shepherds have also done today to the Roman-Catholic Church, the chosen flock of the LORD. Indeed, from the spiritual point of view, excommunication is undoubtedly "a desolate wilderness," since everyone who is out of the Church of Christ lives a fruitless life. But woe to the shepherds who lay waste this sacred heritage of God, because as God has announced, through the Prophet Isaiah, He will drive every rebellious shepherd out of his office, and from his position He will pull him down (cf. Isaiah 22:19). This actually happens at the very moment when a priest profanes the Eucharist, inasmuch as every priest who desecrates the Eucharist is *ipso facto* driven out of his priestly office by virtue of an *automatic excommunication*.

The Prophet Isaiah writes that when "the LORD [will come] out of His place to punish the inhabitants of the earth for their iniquity" (Isaiah 26:21a), then "the earth will also disclose her blood, and will no more cover her slain" (Isaiah 26:21b). And if the earth is to disclose even the blood of slain sinners, which she has soaked up, then she will first of all expose the Most Holy Blood of the *historical* Jesus, the Innocent Blood of the Just One, that has soaked into the earth at the time of the Passion of our LORD, as well as the Most Precious Blood of the *Eucharistic* Jesus, the Divine Blood of the Son of the Living God, that has sacrilegiously been poured into the countless sacrariums and into the ground by rebellious priests. Indeed, the earth is very much imbued with the Innocent Blood of the Lamb of God. When the Blood of Christ was poured into the ground, it was silent; however, when the earth will bring to light the Blood of our LORD, then it will speak mightily on behalf of the faithful ones, but against the rebels. If God listened to the voice of Abel's innocent blood that cried out to Him from the ground (cf. Genesis 4:10c), how much more will He listen to the Most Holy Blood of His Beloved Son, the Most Innocent of all the innocent ones who have ever lived on the earth! If Cain was cursed from the earth (cf. Genesis 4:11), for shedding the innocent blood of his brother, what will be the punishment for those who willfully and intentionally shed the Most Innocent Blood of the Only-Begotten Son of God? "How much worse punishment [...] will he deserve who has trampled under foot the Son of God, profaned the Blood of the Covenant by which he was sanctified, and has insulted the Spirit of Grace?" (Hebrews 10:29). For "the LORD will judge His people" (Hebrews 10:30e). Then "rebels and sinners shall be destroyed together, and those who forsake the LORD shall be consumed" (Isaiah 1:28), and then the LORD will say: "My people have committed two evils: they have forsaken Me, the fountain of living waters, and hewn themselves cisterns – broken cisterns that can hold no water" (Jeremiah 2:13). These two evils are being committed over and over again, when the profanation of the Eucharist takes place, because it is then that the LORD, the fountain of living waters, is forsaken by a lack of faith, and when the sacrariums, which cannot hold the Most Holy Blood of Christ, are used as the instruments, comparable to the broken cisterns, by which the Most Precious Blood of our LORD Jesus Christ is being profaned.

However, what is still more shocking is the fact that those broken cisterns, into which the Most Holy Blood of our LORD is being poured, are not only the sacrariums, but sometimes even ordinary lavatory sinks. When I was serving in a parish – from which I wrote my letter to Joseph Cardinal Ratzinger about the profanation of the Eucharist – it happened that on Easter Sunday 1996, after helping to distribute the Eucharist during the last Mass in the morning, I went to the washroom, which was located right next to the sacristy in our church, and I saw very fresh spots of the Blood of Christ in a regular sink. It was very easy to notice that, because they used a rose wine at Masses. I was devastated, and it caused me to lick the Most Precious Blood of our LORD from the sink. In the rectory, immediately after Mass, I confronted my pastor, who had permitted pouring the Blood of Christ into the sacrarium, informing him about that incident. He became extremely angry; his face turned red, and he yelled at me, saying: "You do not love people;" "you are judgmental."

A few minutes later, I left the rectory and drove on my way to the home of a family who had invited me for dinner. I wept most of the way with my eyes full of bitter tears. There were some moments when I had to slow down, because I felt that I was unable to completely control my driving. When I arrived in the house of my friends, I shared with them my *bad* Easter news which brought me back to Good Friday. My friends were shocked. On that Easter Sunday, when the entire Church joyfully celebrated the Triumph of our LORD over the cross, I personally saw my LORD crucified by His own people. On Easter Morning, while the disciples of Jesus Christ were mourning and weeping, the Risen LORD brought them His peace and joy (cf. Matthew 28:9; Mark 16:10; Luke 24:36.41; John 20:19–21), but on Easter Sunday 1996, I had a "reverse" experience: while I was rejoicing, suddenly my Easter joy turned into mourning and weeping. This was the worst, the darkest and the saddest Easter Sunday of my whole life. I will never forget it.

On a side-note, in this parish the extraordinary Eucharistic ministers, who distributed the Most Precious Blood of our LORD on weekends, used at the liturgy folded gray paper-towels, commonly found in public restrooms, to wipe the rims of the chalices during the distribution of the Blood of Christ, which were later burned. Some of the extraordinary Eucharistic ministers were so careless that they did not even use water to purify the chalices right after the distribution of Holy Communion, but they only wiped the chalices with the afore-mentioned paper-towels and left them in the sacristy of the church; then the chalices were purified after Holy Mass by someone who was in charge of it. The paper-towels with the Blood of Christ, which the extraordinary Eucharistic ministers left in the sacristy, were completely un-protected, and they could easily be thrown into the trash-can by someone who would not know for which purpose they were used. From the aesthetic point of view, it was disgusting and awful to watch these ugly papers which the extraordinary Eucharistic ministers used for the Most Sacred, the Most Noble and the Most Exquisite Banquet, but first of all, it was illicit, because it is prohibited to burn any vestiges of the Most Holy Communion – be it the Consecrated Bread and/ or the Consecrated Wine – in which our LORD Jesus Christ so intensely and ardently burns for us out of His Divine Love that He gives *Himself totally* to us as our spiritual and Life-giving Nourishment. And ironically, this un-acceptable practice was permitted by my low-class pastor who was master of ceremonies at the cathedral. What a farce! Unfortunately I had to work with him, but only for seven months until the time when the letter from Joseph Cardinal Ratzinger arrived in response to my letter of December 8, 1995 (mentioned in my *FOREWORD*) in which I exposed the profanation of the Eucharist practiced by my pastor and by many other pastors in the diocese. The letter from Joseph Cardinal Ratzinger unequivocally condemned all the abuses of the Most Blessed Sacrament of the Eucharist which took place in my parish and throughout the diocese. Then, the liberal priests, who desecrated the Most Precious Blood of Christ, flared up with hatred towards me, saying: "Let us kill the messenger of bad news!"

The rebellious priests, acting in the bosom of the Roman-Catholic Church, have diffused the sacrilegious practice of profaning the Eucharist as a pestilence throughout North America. In this manner, they have disowned their priestly vocation. They were called by Jesus Christ to diffuse "the fragrance of His knowledge in every place. For we are to God the fragrance of Christ among those who are being saved and among those who are perishing" (2 Corinthians 2:14–15), as Saint Paul the Apostle teaches us. However, instead of the fragrance of Christ's knowledge, the rebel priests have spread a vexatious and devastating odor of ignorance, evil and spiritual death. It may be said that they have created a liturgical culture of death. Being inflated with arrogance and pride, the defiant priests have fallen into the demonic snares which they themselves have laid by their disobedience to the teaching of the Church. There are many priests who profane the Eucharist, because they were wrongly educated by other priests, but unfortunately there are also many priests who intentionally elude and repel the law of the Church. Such an attitude is surely demonic! In this way, the impertinent priests lay waste the fruitful fields of the Church's faith. But God will punish those who stubbornly persist in their sins (cf. Psalm 68:22).

The profanation of the Eucharist is a clear sign of the decadence of faith among the clergy and the laity. I do not comprehend at all how priests, who, after being informed that there is an excommunication for pouring the Most Precious Eucharistic Blood of Christ into the sacrarium, can still continue this evil, demonic practice without a qualm. The souls of such priests surely do not serve God, but satan. The Fathers of both the Council of Constance and the Council of Trent introduced the custom of distributing the Eucharist under the form of the Consecrated Bread alone (for lay people and clergy who are not consecrating) for good and serious reasons. And today there is a huge and urgent reason to do the same.

The Wisdom of God says on the pages of Sacred Scripture: "As the people's judge is, so are his officials; as the ruler of the city is, so are all its inhabitants. An undisciplined king ruins his people, but a city becomes fit to live in through the wisdom of its rulers" (Sirach 10:2–3). The profanation of the Eucharist is the best evidence that many of those priests who were made responsible for the People of the Church proved themselves irresponsible and undisciplined rulers who ruined the inhabitants of the City of God. It is high time to re-build the spiritual ruins in the bosom of the Roman-Catholic Church after the devastating ravage caused by the profanation of the Most Holy Eucharist. Using the language of the Council of Basel from Session 1, held on December 14, 1431, we can say that "as the vine of Christ has already almost run wild on account of the multitude of thistles and thorns of vices, [which in our case are surely the acts of the profanation of the Eucharist], crowding in upon it, [the Church must] cut them back through the endeavour of necessary cultivation, with the work from on high of the Evangelical husbandman (cf. John 15:1–2), so that it may flourish again and produce with happy abundance the fruits of virtue and esteem."[101]

The official prohibition of the distribution of the Consecrated Wine for the lay people, following the ecclesiastical prudence of our ancestors in faith, is the best way to stop the profanation of the Most Precious Blood of our LORD Jesus Christ. The fact that "Holy Communion has a fuller form as a sign when it takes place under both kinds"[102] should not be excessively stressed nor dogmatized, since it can by no means be used as the decisive argument in favor of the distribution of the Eucharist under both species. Countless Saints are in Heaven who have never received Holy Communion under both kinds. Therefore, let us not fanatically insist on a "fuller form" of the Eucharist when the Salvation of so many Catholics is at stake. It is not the "fuller form" of the Eucharist that saves, but Jesus Christ Himself when He is received with faith and reverence. It is better to enter Heaven, having not received Holy Communion under the "fuller form" than to go to hell after having received Holy Communion under the "fuller form" followed by its profanation. The Salvation of the People of God is more important than the Eucharist distributed and received under a "fuller form." The full form of the Eucharist is given by our LORD and it must be cherished by all of us, as it truly is in every celebration of Holy Mass, but it is not the goal in itself, inasmuch as Jesus Christ is equally present under the form of the Consecrated Bread, as well as under the form of the Consecrated Wine. The full form of the Eucharist helps us to

---

[101] Ibid., p. 456.
[102] *The Roman Missal*, op. cit., p. 81*.

better understand the *sacrificial* dimension of Holy Communion as the true Body and Blood of our LORD offered for our Salvation; however, a "fuller form" itself is not more important than the Sacredness of the Eucharistic Substance itself which is our Living and Life-giving LORD Himself. It is not the "form" or "sign" that suffers, but Jesus Christ Himself who suffers profanation (cf. Isaiah 48:11b) whenever He is brutally sent to the realm of oblivion by those whom He has loved and for whom He has laid down His Life.

The profanation of the Eucharist is really a nation-wide problem in the Roman-Catholic Church in North America. We should not be naïve that the profanation of the Most Holy Blood of Christ will cease through better education and proper training of the extraordinary Eucharistic ministers, because there will always be many careless ministers who will not protect the Eucharist. This can be proven by one simple fact, namely, that many of those who profane the Eucharist, even when they learn that pouring the Blood of Christ into the sacrarium is strictly prohibited in the Roman-Catholic Church, still continue this demonic practice. The belief that the profanation of the Blood of Christ will cease when all the extraordinary Eucharistic ministers are better prepared for their ministry, can be compared to one who claims that all who practice gluttony will eat less when they are informed that obesity is unhealthy. This is a purely hypothetical idea which is completely out of reality!

The problem of the profanation of the Eucharist must not be ignored nor swept under the carpet, as many of the clergy try to do, and I am reluctant to believe that the bishops themselves will put an end to this crime. The profanation of the Blood of Christ can really be overcome by the strict prohibition of the distribution of the Most Holy Communion under both forms for lay people, following the decrees of the Councils of Constance and Trent. This is the shortest and most effective way to stop this spiritually death-bringing practice, but this issue needs to be addressed *directly* by the Apostolic See. I have no doubt whatsoever that this disease of the profanation of the Eucharist can actually be eradicated, that it can finally be extirpated, *only* by the *official*, *firm* and *steadfast* decision of the Highest Ecclesiastical Authorities, following the Ecumenical Council of Constance which, at Session 13, held on June 15, 1415, unequivocally and categorically prohibited the distribution of the Consecrated Wine for lay people "under pain of excommunication."[103] And I pray God that one day soon this will be done.

---

[103] N. P. Tanner, *vol. I*, op. cit., p. 419.

2.

An Appeal to All Priests Who Profane the Eucharist

*I*n this chapter, I want to address you priests who profaned in the past and you priests who today still profane the Most Holy Sacrament of the Eucharist. I know that many of you, reading the present book, will be very angry, but let no angry word come forth from your mouths. It is not with your anger that you should respond to the message of this book, but with your meditative silence which will lead you to repentance (cf. 2 Corinthians 7:9a). Remember, you have been crucifying your LORD over and over again; you did not betray Him three times as Peter the Apostle – who later repented and was reconciled with Jesus Christ – but possibly three thousand times; however, your LORD, "though He was harshly treated and afflicted, yet He opened not His mouth" (Isaiah 53:7a). And now, you, in turn, open not your mouth, but your hearts, and let your hearts cry out to Jesus Christ: "Spare us, O LORD" (cf. Joel 2,17b). You, rebellious priests, "were like sheep going astray, but [...] now [return] to the Shepherd and Overseer of your souls" (1 Peter 2:25) "with all your heart, with fasting, with weeping, and with mourning" (Joel 2:12b). May your mouths keep silent, but may your hearts speak loudly. So then, open your ears, your minds, your hearts and listen attentively: Your hands are stained with the Most Innocent, the Most Precious and the Most Sacred Blood of our LORD Jesus Christ, "the Son of the Living God" (Matthew 16:16b; cf. John 1:34), "the Lamb of God who takes away the sin of the world" (John 1:29b; cf. 1:36b).

In his First Letter to Timothy, Saint Paul the Apostle expresses the following wish: "I desire that the men pray everywhere, lifting up holy hands ..." (1 Timothy 2:8). All the more the hands of priests are to be holy, and not steeped in the Blood of Christ, because their hands have been sanctified in the Sacrament of Priestly Ordination so as to be like the Hands of Jesus Christ Himself. The hands of priests are to be living vessels in which they are to cherish the Eucharistic LORD; their consecrated hands are to protect the Most Holy Communion, and not to be an instrument of this criminal activity which is the profanation of the Eucharist.

Rebellious priests, our LORD Jesus Christ has chosen your hands to be holy and innocent, but instead, "your hands are full of [His] Blood" (Isaiah 1:15c). Therefore, convert and "draw near to God and He will draw near to you. Cleanse your hands, you sinners; and purify your hearts, you double-minded" (James 4:8). When Cain shed the blood of his brother Abel, God asked him: "What have you done? The voice of your brother's blood cries out to Me from the ground" (Genesis 4:10b.c). And today, God the Father asks all of you, priests, who profane the Most Precious Blood of His Only Begotten Son: "What have you done? The voice of My Beloved Son's Blood cries out to Me from the ground into which you have poured it down mindless of its priceless value paid for your salvation (cf. Genesis

4:10b.c)." Cain shed the blood of man, but you, murderous priests, shed the Blood of the Son of the Living and Life-giving God. This is clearly a demonic activity, and it is hard to believe that the profanation of the Most Holy Blood of Christ has been going on already for a half century! "How long, O you, [insane priests], will you turn [God's] Glory to shame? How long will you love [evil], and seek falsehood?" (Psalm 4:3). Hear, O rebellious priests, and give ear, "for the LORD has spoken: 'I have nourished and brought up children, and they have rebelled against Me'" (Isaiah 1:2b.c). "Woe [to you], sinful [generation], a people laden with iniquity, a brood of evildoers, children who are corrupters! [You] have forsaken the LORD, [you] have provoked to anger the Holy One of Israel, [you] have turned away backward. Why should you be stricken again? Why do you continue to revolt?" (Isaiah 1:4–5b). "A son honors his father, and a servant his master. If, then, I am the Father, where is My Honor? And if I am a Master, where is My Reverence? Says the LORD of Hosts to you priests who despise My Name. Yet you say, 'In what way have we despised Your Name?'" (Malachi 1:6). You despise My Name by profaning the Most Holy Blood of My Son whom I have highly exalted and bestowed on Him the Name which is above every other name, so that at the Name of My Son every knee must bow, of those in Heaven, and of those on earth, and of those under the earth (cf. Philippians 2:9–10); you despise My Name by saying that the left-over Blood of My Beloved Son, which He shed on the Altar of the Cross for your salvation, may be poured into the sacrarium, and so be slighted (cf. Malachi 1:7c); you despise My Name when you are mindless of My Son really present in the Eucharist in whom you "have Redemption through His Blood, the forgiveness of sins, according to the riches of His Grace" (Ephesians 1:7). "By Him [I have reconciled] all things to [Myself], by Him, whether things on earth or things in heaven, having made peace through the Blood of His Cross" (Colossians 1:20), but you are crucifying My Beloved Son over and over again. A mercenary would be more mindful of the Eucharist than you stiff-necked priests who are to care *ex officio* for My Son present in this Blessed Sacrament. Therefore, "I have no pleasure in you [...], and I will not accept an offering from your hands" (Malachi 1:10b). Yes, God does not want any offering from your hands: firstly, because you do not believe in the real presence of Jesus Christ in Holy Communion, which results in your profanation of this Most Holy Sacrament, and secondly, because you who desecrate the Eucharist are excommunicated, and consequently, you must NOT celebrate Mass. Therefore, thus says the LORD through the Prophet Isaiah: "When you spread out your hands, I will hide My eyes from you; even though you make many prayers, I will not hear. Your hands are full of blood. Wash yourselves, make yourselves clean; put away the evil of your doings from before My eyes. Cease to do evil" (Isaiah 1:15–16). Therefore, cleanse your hands of the Blood of Christ – that you shed by your criminal deeds – so that they may become innocent anew, and serve as portable shelters and tabernacles for your LORD, inasmuch as the Most Precious Blood of Christ is to be *in*, and not *on* your hands. It was not the *outer*, but the *inner* part of your hands that was anointed, when you were ordained, and when Jesus Christ was laid in your consecrated, priestly hands as in a manger to be wrapped in the cloths of your faith and love (cf. Luke 2:7), but instead, you stripped Him through your lack of faith and love (cf. Matthew 27:28), and you shed the Blood of your Brother "according to the flesh, [the Blood of] the Christ [...] who is over all, God blessed forever. AMEN" (Romans 9:5).

However, through the service of the Church, Jesus Christ has placed Himself not only in your hands, but also in your minds and hearts, entrusting you with the task of the correct, true, genuine teaching and the sound pastoral leadership which must always be in accord with the will of God and the law of the Church, but you have misled the People of God and led them astray. You have not attended to the words of God spoken through the Prophet Malachi: "The lips of the priest are to keep knowledge, and people are to seek the law from his mouth, because he is the messenger of the LORD of Hosts. But you have turned aside from the way [of the LORD], and you have caused many to stumble by your instruction [...]. Therefore, I also have made you contemptible and base before all the people, since you have not kept My ways ..." (Malachi 2:7–8a.9). How timely are these words today, as though they were written for you, unlearned contemporary priests, who turn aside from the right way of God and of His Holy Church, by your desecration of the Eucharist, and cause many to falter by your wrong instruction. You forfeit your own lives and the lives of those who, trusting you as the chosen vicars of Christ, follow you. How brutally you weaken the faith of so many Catholics! Who is able to count all the innocent and single-hearted altar-boys and altar-girls who have been scandalized and wounded, in the span of a half century, by seeing the deacons and the extraordinary Eucharistic ministers pour the Most Precious Blood of Christ into the sacrarium? How many of those innocent and single-minded children lost their faith forever in the real presence of Jesus Christ in the Eucharist? How many hearts of the parents of altar-boys and altar-girls have been broken after they heard from their children about the profanation of the Most Holy Communion? Have you ever thought, you rebels, that when profaning the Eucharist you were at the service of satan, the author of chaos and confusion? You have brought about divisions in the very bosom of the Roman-Catholic Church, your Spiritual Mother, because you did not follow the Spirit of God (cf. Jude 19), and you did not obey the Authorities of the Roman-Catholic Church. In this manner, you have killed the faith of those whose faith you were to cherish and to strengthen. Come to your senses! "Do not quench the Spirit" (1 Thessalonians 5:19), for "God yearns jealously for the Spirit that He has made to dwell in us" (James 4:5b; cf. Exodus 20:5b). Therefore, "do not grieve the Holy Spirit of God, by whom you were sealed for the Day of Redemption" (Ephesians 4:30), "but always pursue what is good both for yourselves and for all" (1 Thessalonians 5:15). Open your minds and hearts to the Holy Spirit, "for all who are led by the Spirit of God are children of God" (Romans 8:14). Stop serving the devil! Serve God alone! Burn up the letter of satan, written with the ink of your evil deeds, and begin to minister a new epistle of Christ, written by the Spirit of the Living God on the tablets of the hearts of the faithful (cf. 2 Corinthians 3:3). However, in order to form the hearts of others, the shepherds themselves must have hearts molded according to the Most Sacred Heart of Jesus. Already in the times of the Old Testament, God made a firm promise to His people, saying: "I will give you shepherds according to My heart, who will feed you with knowledge and understanding" (Jeremiah 3:15). "'And now, O priests, this commandment is for you. If you will not hear, and if you will not take it to heart, to give Glory to My Name,' says the LORD of Hosts, 'I will send a curse upon you, and I will curse your blessings. Yes, I have cursed them already, because you do not take it to heart'" (Malachi 2:1–2). For "the curse of the LORD is on the house of the wicked, but He blesses the dwelling of the righteous" (Proverbs 3:33).

So then, first renew your hearts in the LORD, then "amend your ways and your doings" (Jeremiah 7:3b), and your curse will turn into God's Blessing.

There is no doubt whatsoever that you have turned aside from the way of God due to your lack of faith in the Eucharist, and you have caused many to stumble by your false instruction because of your arrogance, ignorance and lack of knowledge. You did not follow the Biblical advice: "Before you speak, learn" (Sirach 18:19a), and before you celebrate the Eucharist, believe. But you acted conversely, by speaking and teaching others wrongly, not learning first what is right. You are like those about whom the Wisdom of God says in the Book of Proverbs: "Because they hated knowledge and did not choose the fear of the LORD, they would have none of my counsel and despised my every rebuke" (Proverbs 1:29–30). Therefore, being without knowledge, you "are blind leaders of the blind" (Matthew 15:14b), and because you are blind, you blind others and both of you fall into a ditch (cf. Matthew 15:14c; Luke 6:39b.c; 2 Peter 1:9; Revelation 3:17). The Second Vatican Council in Chapter 14 of its *Constitution on the Sacred Liturgy*, promulgated at Session 3 held on December 4, 1963, says that "those who are responsible for pastoral care [must] first get thoroughly immersed in the spirit and power of the liturgy themselves, and become competent in it."[104] Needless to say, you, indeed, are *in*-competent in your priestly ministry.

God did not call you to lead His People into a spiritual ditch, but to lay hold of them and lift them out of it when they fall into it, as well as to build them up spiritually. But it was you yourselves who have fallen into a deadly ditch and have dragged down many together with you. So now you are in a ditch, confused and at a loss. However, bear in mind that you

---

[104] Ibid., *vol. II*, p. 824.

are called by the Heavenly Father to the noblest task on earth to continue to build up the Mystical Body of the Church in the Name of Jesus Christ, His Beloved Son, "in whom the whole building, being joined together, grows into a holy temple in the LORD, in whom you also are being built together for a dwelling place of God in the Spirit" (Ephesians 2:21–22). The Heavenly Father called you to suffer with His Son, not to crucify Him over and over again. But you put yourselves among the chief priests, the elders, the scribes and the crowds, and you crucify our LORD (cf. Matthew 27:12.22–23.25; Mark 15:1.3.13–14; Luke 23:1.21.23; John 19:6). The Heavenly Father called you to stay awake with His Son in the Garden of Gethsemani (cf. Matthew 26:36–46; Mark 14:32–42; Luke 22:39–46); He called you to carry the cross of His Son together with Him, and not as Simon the Cyrenean who was forced to bear the cross of Jesus (cf. Matthew 27:32; Mark 15:21; Luke 23:26), but willingly (cf. Matthew 10:38; 16:24b; Mark 8:34b; Luke 9:23b; 14:27). The Heavenly Father called you to stand at the foot of the Cross of His Beloved Son together with the Most Blessed Mary, the Mother of our LORD, with Saint John the Apostle and with many others who followed Jesus (cf. Matthew 27:55–56; Mark 15:40–41; Luke 23:49; John 19:25–27), not with those who crucified Him. You are called to be faithful and trustworthy servants of Christ and stewards of the Mysteries of God (cf. 1 Corinthians 4:1–2), but instead of being faithful and trustworthy ministers of our LORD, you prove yourselves *un*-faithful and *un*-trustworthy by your ignorance and arrogance, and instead of building up the Church, the Mystical Body of Christ, you crucify His Body and you open the wounds of Jesus over and over again, when you profane the Eucharist. The Prophet Isaiah writes that "by His wounds we are healed"

(Isaiah 53:5b). The wounds of Jesus Christ are to be kissed with faith and love, not to be opened over and over again.

You are to be a part of the building process of the Church, the Sacred Heritage of the LORD, following the example of the Apostles who did not profane the Blood of Christ, but shed and mingled their own blood with that of Jesus. "And they defeated [the devil] by the Blood of the Lamb and by the word of their testimony, and they did not love their lives to the death (Revelation 12:11). By their martyrdom, they strengthened the faith of the People of God, following the example of Saint Peter the Apostle (cf. Luke 22:31–32; John 21:15–19), but you cooperate with the devil, and you weaken the faith of many Catholics, when you desecrate the Eucharist; in this way, you sift them as wheat. You imitate satan, by your demonic practices, about whom our LORD said that he "has asked to sift [the Apostles] as wheat" (Luke 22:31b). "O you, *dis*-grace to your Master's house!" (Isaiah 22:18b), you, who sacrilegiously steal the Most Precious Blood of Christ and pour it into the sacrarium and into the ground. You act as those about whom Saint Peter the Apostle writes: "These men pour abuse on things of which they are ignorant. They act like irrational animals, like natural brute beasts ..." (2 Peter 2:12). That's how you make of the House of God "a den of thieves" (Matthew 21:13b; Mark 11:17b; Luke 19:46b; John 2:16b; cf. Isaiah 56:7; Jeremiah 7,11). Therefore, you are driven out of the Roman-Catholic Church with the ecclesial whip of cords which is your *excommunication* (cf. John 2:15). Then how can you be the spiritual builders of the Mother Church if you do not remain lawfully in her bosom? Keep in mind that your lack of faith and fidelity is not only your personal problem. As false shepherds in the flock of Christ, you weaken the faith of those to whom you are sent by your LORD. In this way, you imitate the wickedness of the scribes and Pharisees to whom Jesus addressed the following words: "Woe to you, scribes and Pharisees, hypocrites! For you shut off the Kingdom of Heaven from men; for you neither go in yourselves, nor do you allow those who are entering to go in" (Matthew 23:13).

Remember that God called you to be His fellow workers in building up His Church (cf. 1 Corinthians 3:9a). According to the Grace of God which was given to you, you are to be God's wise master builders who build on the foundation laid by Jesus Christ Himself (cf. 1 Corinthians 3:10a). And the Apostle Paul exhorts all those who are in charge of building up the Household of God with the following words: "Let each one take heed how he builds on [this foundation]. For no other foundation can anyone lay than that which is laid, which is Jesus Christ" (1 Corinthians 3:10b–11). Now, I am asking you: How can you be God's fellow workers; how can you be His wise master builders, when you – instead of building on the foundation, which is Jesus Christ – destroy the faith of the faithful in the real presence of Jesus Christ in the Eucharist, by pouring His Most Precious Blood into the sacrarium, this Priceless Blood which is the *VERY FOUNDATION* of the Holy Church of God, and on which His Church has been built? How can you build up the Church of Christ, when you act so basely against your Divine Master and LORD? "Do you not know that you are the temple of God and that the Spirit of God dwells in you? If anyone defiles the temple of God, God will destroy him. For the temple of God is holy, and you are that temple" (1 Corinthians 3:16–17). But you lay waste the living temple of God in the hearts of so many Catholics. You, priests, are called to be spiritual fathers to the faithful, but you, who profane the Eucharist, are rather step-fathers who do not care for your spiritual sons and daughters. Therefore, attend to the words of Saint Paul the Apostle who has said: "But

I discipline my body and bring it into subjection, lest, when I have preached to others, I myself should be rejected" (1 Corinthians 9:27). You need not only to discipline your body, as the shepherds of the flock of Jesus Christ, but your mind as well. Do not be men of depraved, corrupt, ruined mind (cf. 1 Timothy 6:5; 2 Timothy 3:8); do not be men of debased, reprobate mind (Romans 1:28), but *metanoeite* – "change your mind" (Matthew 3:2b; 4:17b; Mark 1:15c) in accordance with the will of the Church, and you will have "the mind of Christ" (1 Corinthians 2:16b) who is "the Head of the Body, the Church" (Colossians 1:18). And the mind of Christ and the mind of His Holy Church are one in saying to you: *It is strictly prohibited to pour the Most Holy Blood of the Incarnate Son of God into the ground or into the sacrarium.* Such is the mind of Christ expressed by the collective mind of the Church. Once you have the mind of Christ and of His Holy Church, you will be at peace with yourselves and with the entire Church, "and the peace of God, which surpasses all understanding, will guard your hearts and minds through Christ Jesus (Philippians 4:7). Then you will not "sit in darkness and the shadow of death" (Luke 1:79), because the LORD will raise you up, and redeem you for His mercies' sake (cf. Psalm 44:27), and He will "guide [your] feet into the way of peace" (Luke 1:79), peace of mind and peace of heart.

The Apostle Paul teaches that "anyone who does not have the Spirit of Christ does not belong to Him" (Romans 8:9b). Indeed, those who profane the Eucharist do not have the Spirit of Christ, and they do not belong to Him, because everyone who has the Spirit of Christ must simultaneously have a profound reverence for the Eucharist, inasmuch as the Spirit of Christ and the Eucharist constitute one indivisible Divine reality. And because you do not have the Spirit of Christ, you deceive the deacons and the extraordinary Eucharistic ministers, when you falsely instruct them to pour the Most Precious Blood of Christ into the sacrarium, saying: "That's what the sacrarium is for." You do it, because you have no faith in the real presence of Jesus Christ in the Eucharist. You spread this evil teaching which comes from your evil hearts. "Brood of vipers! How can you speak good things, when you are evil? For out of the abundance of the heart the mouth speaks" (Matthew 12:34; cf. Luke 6:45c). And what is the abundance of the hearts of those who profane the Eucharist and bid others to do the same? The abundance of their hearts is "a noisy gong [and] a clanging cymbal" (1 Corinthians 13:1); it is a demonic jabber of evil; it is a whisper of the devil himself. That your teaching is evil and demonic is confirmed by the fact that the profanation of the Most Holy Eucharist incurs an automatic *excommunication*! And the evil of your profanation of the Eucharist has its roots in the evil which dwells in your hearts, because you disown the truth about the Eucharist and the authority of the juridical regulations of the Roman-Catholic Church which unequivocally, firmly and steadfastly prohibit pouring the left-over Blood of Christ into the sacrarium.

"If you are willing and obedient, you [will find the way back to God]; but if you refuse and rebel, you shall be devoured by the sword [of His wrath]" (Isaiah 1:19–20a). Return, then, to the LORD that you may live, and not perish. Admit to your evildoing, confess that you have greatly sinned, and cry out to the LORD with the words of the Psalmist: "Our soul is bowed down to the dust; our body clings to the ground. Arise for our help, and redeem us for Your mercies' sake" (Psalm 44:26–27). Yes, may your soul bow down to the dust; may your body cling to the ground into which you have poured the rivers of the Most Holy and Life-giving Blood of Christ, and pay heed to "the voice of your [Divine] Brother's

Blood [that] cries out to [you] from the ground" (Genesis 4:10c). "See to it that you do not refuse Him who is speaking" (Hebrews 12:25a); do not be deaf to His voice, because it will be the same voice that on the Day of the Last Judgment will pierce the hearts of all, when our Divine King will say to those at His right hand: "Come, you blessed of My Father, inherit the kingdom prepared for you from the foundation of the world" (Matthew 25:34b), while to those at His left hand He will say: "Depart from Me, you cursed, into the everlasting fire prepared for the devil and his angels" (Matthew 25:41b). Therefore, be intent on what the voice of Jesus Christ whispers today to the ears of your conscience, as the Prophet Elijah listened to "a gentle whisper [of God]" (1 Kings 19:12), and obey this voice before it thunders out on the Day of the Last Judgment. Then, "the voice of the LORD [will flash] forth flames of fire" (Psalm 29:7), "for indeed our God is a consuming fire" (Hebrews 12:29). He Himself has promised, saying: "I will shake the heavens and the earth and the sea and the dry land; and I will shake all the nations ..." (Haggai 2:6b–7a; cf. Hebrews 12:26). "It is a fearful thing to fall into the hands of the Living God" (Hebrews 10:31). Therefore, "today, if you hear His voice, do not harden your hearts ..." (Psalm 95:7b–8; cf. Hebrews 3:7b.15b; 4:7b), as in the days when you desecrated the Eucharist; otherwise, "[being] hardened through the deceitfulness of sin" (Hebrews 3:13), you "shall not enter [God's] rest" (Psalm 95:11b) "because of [your] unbelief" (Hebrews 3:19). "Beware, brethren, lest there be in any of you an evil heart of unbelief in departing from the Living God" (Hebrews 3:12). "Therefore, since a promise remains of entering His rest, let us fear lest any of you seem to have come short of it" (Hebrews 4:1). "Therefore, submit to God" (James 4:7a), "for [...] he who humbles himself will be exalted" (Matthew 23:12), and un-tie the damnable manacles of your excommunication by your repentance and penance; "you, being dead in your trespasses" (Colossians 2:13), return to Jesus Christ. He will forgive you all your evildoing; He will cancel out your un-payable debt that is against you, and He, the LORD, will make you alive together with Him (cf. Colossians 2:13–14), but "only acknowledge your iniquity, that you have rebelled against the LORD, your God ..." (Jeremiah 3:13a). Have courage, you, "who [walk] in darkness [...], who [dwell] in the land of the shadow of death" (Isaiah 9:1; cf. Luke 1:79). "Awake, you who sleep, arise from the dead, and Christ will give you light" (Ephesians 5:14b).

Think of the terrible crime to which you have succumbed by your lack of faith in the Eucharistic Jesus Christ and by your sacrilegious practices, when you were sending our LORD into the depths of the earth. "You have condemned, you have murdered the Just; He does not resist you" (James 5:6). When you were pouring the Most Holy Blood of Christ into the sacrarium, through the hands of the extraordinary ministers of the Eucharist, then our LORD "was harshly treated and afflicted, yet He opened not His mouth; He was led as a lamb to the slaughter, and as a sheep before its shearers is silent, so He opened not His mouth" (Isaiah 53:7; cf. Matthew 26:63a; Acts 8:32b.c). Each Sunday, after Mass, you go out to shake the hands of the people with your faces looking happy; you are smiling and chatting with your parishioners, being completely indifferent to and mindless of the desecration of the Most Holy Eucharist which took place just a few minutes ago. Then, you go home or you visit your friends, and you enjoy "the Day the LORD has made" (Psalm 118:24a), the Day when Jesus Christ rose from the dead (cf. 1 Thessalonians 4:14), but the Originator of this Glorious Day, you first crucify over and over again, sending Him into "the land of oblivion" (Psalm 88:13b), the One who is "the Author of

Life" (Acts 3:15) and most worthy of our honor and loving memory. The Heavenly Father raised His Son up, "having loosed the pains of death" (Acts 2:24), but you tie the pains of death again, when you profane the Most Holy Eucharistic Blood of His Beloved Son. And all this ironically happens on the Day of the Resurrection of our LORD, exactly on the Day of His Triumph over death. Instead of participating in His Gift of Eternal Life, you bring death upon yourselves and upon those who with you commit the crime of the profanation of the Eucharist. Shame on you! You despise Jesus Christ from whom you received the undeserved honor and privilege of sharing in His Divine Priesthood. The Divine Host invites to His Eucharistic Banquet you who are His "useless servants" (Luke 17:10b), and who are to do what is your duty (cf. Luke 17:10c). And what do you do? You recline at the Eucharistic Table, but once you are nourished by the Divine Host, you throw Him away. No wonder that "what you desire you do not obtain" (James 4:2a), because you do not gather with Christ and His Holy Church, but you scatter (cf. Matthew 12:30; Luke 11:23), being empty intellectually and spiritually, and stripped of the Grace of God, since that's what the *excommunication* is all about. You squander the Divine Endowment which our LORD has granted to you as – HIS FREE GIFT!

He has sent you to increase, not to decrease the number of His followers, and to teach them to observe all things that He has commanded you through His Holy Church; instead, you scandalize and spiritually kill the disciples of Jesus Christ. Therefore, God rebukes you through the Prophet Ezekiel, saying: "The weak you have not strengthened, nor have you healed those who were sick, nor bound up the broken, nor brought back what was driven away, nor sought what was lost; but with force and cruelty you have ruled them" (Ezekiel 34:4). And how cruel was your rule, O you wicked and rebellious pastors, when, abusing your priestly authority and the People of God who put their trust in you as pastors, you forced your associate pastors, deacons and extraordinary Eucharistic ministers to pour the Most Holy Blood of our LORD Jesus Christ into the sacrarium! That's exactly what, in your particular case, the words: "With force and cruelty you have ruled them" mean. You did not strengthen their weak faith, but made it still weaker; you did not heal the wounds of their sins, but you wounded their souls even more by forcing them to desecrate the Eucharist, and even when you learned that pouring the Blood of Christ into the sacrarium is strictly prohibited in the Church under pain of excommunication, you did not bind up the broken by asking the Apostolic See for an absolution for them; you did not bring back what had been driven away, nor did you seek what had been lost by your wrong instruction – and this you could do by re-educating them that after the distribution of the Eucharist the remaining Blood of our LORD must be immediately and completely consumed – but you left them alone without any spiritual help, confused as they are now. Jesus Christ called you to "seek what was lost and bring back what was driven away, bind up the broken and strengthen what was sick" (Ezekiel 34:16a; cf. John 3:17), following His example who "has come to seek and to save that which was lost" (Luke 19:10); you are called by our LORD to be spiritual physicians for His people (cf. Matthew 9:12b; Mark 2:17b; Luke 5:31b), but you are their killers. Shame on you! Your spiritual callousness and induration are loathsome. Therefore, Jesus Christ rebukes you, saying: "I have this against you that you have forsaken your first love" (Revelation 2:4). Thus, "repent and do the first works" (Revelation 2:5b), if you want "to eat from the tree of life, which is in the midst of the Paradise of God" (Revelation 2:7b; cf. 22:14.19; Genesis 2:9). "'For I have no pleasure in the death of one who dies,' says the LORD God. 'Therefore, turn and live!'" (Ezekiel 18:32).

At the time of the Old Testament, God addressed His people, through the Prophet Micah, saying: "O My people, what have I done to you? And how have I wearied you? Answer Me" (Micah 6:3; cf. Jeremiah 2:5). Today, God asks you the same rhetorical questions: "O My priests, what have I done to you? And how have I wearied you?" You had slept in the dust of the earth, and I have awaked you to Everlasting Life (cf. Daniel 12:2). You, however, put Me down over and over again into the dust of the earth, into the place of oblivion (cf. Psalm 88:13b). "[I] have made [you] a little lower than the Angels, and [I] have crowned [you] with glory and honor. [I] have made [you] to have dominion over the works of [My] hands; [I] have put all things under [your] feet" (Psalm 8:6–7), and I have even given you My own Son whom I "did not spare [...], but delivered Him up for [you] all ..." (Romans 8:32). In turn, My Son has totally offered Himself for your Salvation on the Altar of the Cross, and, in His Ultimate and Inexpressible Generosity, He has remained with you in the Most Blessed Sacrament of His Body and Blood, but your closed hearts are mindless of His Most Sacred Heart always opened to you.

The Eucharistic Jesus Christ is the Last Will, the Eternal Testament of the Heavenly Father given to the Church. The Incarnate Son of God, present in the Sacrament of Holy Communion, is our Priceless Spiritual Endowment, sealed with His Own and Most Sacred Blood. And when you, priests, desecrate the Sacrament of the Eucharist, you squander the Most Precious, Living and Life-giving Heavenly Treasure, bestowed on the Church by God the Father. The one who is prodigal of this Most Sacred, Divine Gift resembles the Biblical prodigal son. He should not tend the flock of Christ, but instead he should be sent into the fields to feed swine (cf. Luke 15:15), and "to fill his stomach with the pods that the pigs [eat] …" (Luke 15:16). Perhaps then, he would come to his senses, and say (cf. Luke 15:17a): "How many of my Father's hired servants have more than enough [Eucharistic] Bread, while I am dying here with [spiritual] hunger! I will arise and go to my Father, and will say to Him, 'Father, I have sinned against heaven and before You, and I am no longer worthy to be called Your son. Make me like one of Your hired servants'" (Luke 15:17b–19). All you who profane the Most Holy Blood of Christ come to your senses, and leave the "fields of unclean swine," that is to say, the desolate fields and aimless paths of sin and spiritual defilement, the fields outside the Mother Church which are technically called – *excommunication*.

You profane the Blood of the Incarnate Son of God, the Divine Power of your exaltation and exultation, that has made you adopted sons of the Heavenly Father. Jesus Christ shed His Blood to save you, but you shed His Blood sacrilegiously to condemn yourselves and those who follow your insanity. What ingratitude! Shame on you! Even unbelieving hirelings would have more respect for the Eucharist than you who are called by our LORD to be, *ex professo* and by virtue of your priestly office, the servants of His Altar. In his Letter to the Ephesians, the Apostle Paul writes that "[Jesus Christ] Himself gave some to be Apostles, some Prophets, some Evangelists, and some pastors and teachers, for the equipping of the saints for the work of ministry, for the edifying of the Body of Christ, till we all come to the unity of the faith and of the knowledge of the Son of God, to a perfect man, to the measure of the stature of the fullness of Christ" (Ephesians 4:11–13). And again, the said Apostle teaches that the Church is "built on the foundation of the Apostles and Prophets [with] Jesus Christ

Himself [as] the chief corner-stone" (Ephesians 2:20). Saint Paul assures you that "the God and Father of our LORD Jesus Christ [...] has bestowed on [you] in Christ every spiritual blessing in the Heavens. God chose [you] in Him before the world began to be holy and blameless in His sight in love" (Ephesians 1:3–4); the Heavenly Father "raised [you] up together, and made [you] sit together in the Heavens in Christ Jesus" (Ephesians 2:6). "And we know that all things work together for good to those who love God, who are called according to His purpose. For whom He foreknew, He also predestined to be conformed to the image of His Son, that He might be the First-born among many brethren. Moreover, whom He predestined, these He also called; whom He called, these He also justified; and whom He justified, these He also glorified" (Romans 8:28–30).

Consider all these gifts that God bestowed on you *through* and *in* His Only Begotten Son, and think of what you have done to Him, when you desecrated His Most Sacred Blood. In addition to all these graces, adduced above from the letters of Saint Paul, God conferred on you one more and extraordinary grace, when He called you to be partakers of the hierarchical Priesthood of His Son. However, you have squandered all these fully undeserved gifts by one single act of the profanation of the Eucharist! Shame on you! Ponder – and not only for a moment, but at every moment of your life – how great is the dignity to which you were called by the Heavenly Father in His Only Begotten and Most Beloved Son Jesus Christ, and how Precious is the Blood of our LORD, the Blood of the unblemished and spotless Lamb of God beyond all price (cf. 1 Peter 1:19), by which "you may be partakers of the Divine Nature" (2 Peter 1:4). "Fix [your] attention on the Blood of Christ and recognize how Precious it is to God His Father, since it was shed for our Salvation and brought the grace of repentance to all the world,"[105] as Saint Clement writes. If the Blood of Christ had been so Precious to you as it is to God His Father, you would never have profaned it. May the Saving Blood of our LORD also incline your minds and hearts to a profound repentance, because the Heavenly Father has lifted you up on high *through* the Most Precious Blood of His own Son; He has brought you up *in* Him to the highest realm of existence, but through your unfaithfulness and rebellious attitude toward the will of God and of His Holy Church, you have brought yourselves down low to the dust of spiritual death (cf. Psalm 44:26a) by your sacrilegious act of the profanation of the Most Sacred Blood of Christ. The Blood of our Savior that has sent you to Heaven, making you partakers of His Divine Nature, you send over and over again into the ground by pouring it into the sacrarium. Over and over again, you brutally dispose of the Priceless Blood of Christ, as though it were worth less than Judas' thirty pieces of silver which he had taken for the Innocent Blood of Jesus (cf. Matthew 26:15b; Exodus 21:32), because I do not believe that having thirty pieces of silver you would get rid of them by throwing them down into the drain. Would you? Saint Matthew the Evangelist relates that "when Judas, who had betrayed [Jesus], saw that He had been condemned, he was seized with remorse and brought back the thirty pieces of silver to the chief priests and the elders, saying, 'I have sinned by betraying Innocent Blood.' [...] Then, he flung the pieces of silver into the temple and departed, and went and hanged himself" (Matthew 27:3–4a.5). Judas flung the thirty pieces of silver *into* the temple, but you, the priests of Christ, take the Most Precious Blood of our Savior *from* His Temple, and you fling it out *into* the ground. Shame

---

[105] "From a letter to the Corinthians by Saint Clement, pope," [in]: *The Liturgy of the Hours, vol. II* (New York 1976), p. 51.

on you! You are worse than Judas! Shame on you! He deeply regretted his evil deed, but you do not regret yours. Judas despised the *soulless* money, taken for the Life of Jesus, but you despise the *Living* and *Life-giving* LORD. You would not throw your money into a trash-can, but without a moment of hesitation you throw our Savior into the ground. Our Divine Master says in His Gospel: "Where your treasure is, there your heart will be also" (Matthew 6:21; Luke 12:34). I am asking all of you who pour the Most Holy Blood of Christ into the sacrarium: Is this the way you should treat our LORD who is the Most Precious Treasure man has ever received from the Heavenly Father? Is the Eucharistic Jesus really *your* treasure? Do you insist that the pouring of the Most Holy Blood of Christ into the ground is a right practice? Then do exactly the same with your most valuable and expensive goods. Put them in the ground and forget about them forever, just as you do with the Most Holy Blood of our LORD Jesus Christ. Judas hated the mammon which he took for Jesus' crucifixion, and he flung it away, but you do not hate the "mammon" of your heretical and sacrilegious practice of profaning the Eucharist, and you do not want to fling away your thirty pieces of silver, that is to say, your demonic pride, but you keep them by crucifying our LORD over and over again whenever you pour His Most Holy and Most Precious Blood into the sacrarium. You arrogantly fling caution to the winds, and you fling dirt at our LORD, by sending Him into the ground. Fling the "evil of your thirty pieces of silver" out of the "window of your unbelief" and believe in the real presence of the Incarnate Son of God in the Eucharist, then you will never crucify Him again. God says through the Prophet Malachi: "Will a man rob God? Yet you have robbed Me!" (Malachi 3:8a.b). Indeed, you have robbed God by your sacrilegious practice of profaning the Most Holy Blood of Christ, inasmuch as this is exactly what the sacrilege is all about, namely, it is "the crime of stealing, misusing, violating, or desecrating that which is sacred, holy, or dedicated to sacred uses."[106] Stop this spiritual robbery immediately, and do not think that you can profane the Eucharist with impunity, "for whatever a man sows, that he will also reap" (Galatians 6:7b). And the harvest, which you reap now, is the burning wrath of God. But if you want to escape your eternal punishment and to reap the Harvest of Eternal Life, take as an example the attitude of "the king of Nineveh [who] arose from his throne and laid aside his robe, covered himself with sackcloth and sat in ashes" (Jonah 3:6). Then, he said: "Who knows? God may turn and relent, and turn away from His fierce anger so that we may not perish" (Jonah 3:9). And as Scripture goes on: "When God saw their deeds, that they turned from their wicked way, then God relented from the disaster that He had said He would bring upon them, and He did not do it" (Jonah 3:10). Therefore, do the following: (1) rise from the throne of your pride; (2) stop the liturgical blood-bath, this cruel liturgical butchery; (3) "Take off the filthy garments from [yourselves]" (Zechariah 3:4b) which are the garments of evil; (4) wash your hands stained with the Innocent Blood of Jesus Christ; (5) cover yourself with the sackcloth of repentance; (6) sit in the ashes of penance; and (7) fast, mourn and weep with a humbled and contrite heart, saying: "Who knows? God may turn and relent, and turn away from His fierce anger so that we may not perish" (Jonah 3:9). For "He scorns the scornful, but gives grace to the humble" (Proverbs 3:34; cf. James 4:6c). And when God sees your conversion how you turned from your evil way, then God will relent from the calamity that you deserve due to your profanation of the Eucharist, and He will not carry it out (cf. Jonah 3:10).

---

[106] P. B. Gove, op. cit., p. 1996.

On the pages of the Old Testament, God cries out through the Prophet Jeremiah, saying: "Stand in the ways and see, and ask for the old paths, where the good way is, and walk in it; then you will find rest for your souls. But they said, 'We will not walk in it'" (Jeremiah 6:16). This is exactly what you, rebellious priests, who profane the Most Holy Blood of Christ, are doing; "you have departed from the [right] way; you have caused many to stumble at the Law. You have corrupted the Covenant of [the LORD]" (Malachi 2:8). For us Catholics, the good way in which to walk is Jesus Christ Himself who guides us by the Authority of the Holy Fathers, the Teaching of the Church and the Law of the Church. These are the ways of the LORD, these are His paths along which we are to walk. Therefore, all you who profane the Most Holy Blood of Christ, abandon the way which leads to hell, and return to Jesus Christ who is "the way, the truth, and the life" (John 14:6b). Rid yourselves of the sister of death and be re-united with your Brother of Life, saying: "Jesus, I am no longer worthy to be called Your brother (cf. Luke 15:19a.21b), but be merciful to me a great sinner (cf. Luke 18:13b) and deliver me from the criminal guilt of shedding Your Most Holy Blood (cf. Psalm 51:16a)." Yes, if you return to Jesus Christ in the spirit of compunction, with your humbled and contrite heart, He will not spurn you (cf. Psalm 51:19), because He "is gracious and merciful, slow to anger and great in mercy" (Psalm 145:8; cf. Exodus 20:6; 34:6–7; Numbers 14:18; Deuteronomy 5:10). Jesus will not bring out a fine robe in order to put it on you, nor will He put a ring on your hand and sandals on your feet, nor will He bring the fatted calf and kill it for a banquet with you as the father of the prodigal son did (cf. Luke 15:22b–23). No, He will not bring out a perishable robe so as to put it on you, nor will He put a golden ring on your hand and sandals on your bare feet. But if you sincerely repent and confess your sins of the profanation of the Eucharist, then the LORD "[will clothe you] with the garments of salvation, He [will cover you] with the robe of righteousness, as a bridegroom decks himself with ornaments, and as a bride adorns herself with her jewels" (Isaiah 61:10b). Then, you will again be the priests of the LORD "clothed with righteousness" (Psalm 132:9) and "with salvation" (2 Chronicles 6:41b; Psalm 132:16); then "[you] will greatly rejoice in the LORD, [your] soul shall be joyful in [your] God" (Isaiah 61:10a), and you will "shout aloud for joy" (Psalm 132:16; see also verse 9). Then, your blood-stained hands will be perfectly cleansed by God's Mercy; then, your sackcloth of repentance will be removed, and the Angel of the LORD "will clothe you with festal robes" (Zechariah 3:4d), not stained with blood, but "washed [...] and made [...] white in the Blood of the Lamb" (Revelation 7:14d), for God promises you through the Prophet Isaiah: "Though your sins are like scarlet, they shall be as white as snow; though they are red like crimson, they shall be as wool" (Isaiah 1:18c.d), and you will be "clothed with white robes, holding palm branches in [your] hands" (Revelation 7:9); then, the ashes of your penance will finally be shaken off you. And when the LORD will wash you in the saving water; yes, when He will thoroughly wash off the blood from you (cf. Ezekiel 16:9), and anoint your head with His holy oil (cf. Psalm 23:5b; Psalm 89:21), then, "it shall come to pass in that day that [the] burden will be taken away from your shoulder, and [the] yoke from your neck, and the yoke will be destroyed because of the anointing oil" (Isaiah 10:27). Then also the words of Saint Paul the Apostle will be fulfilled in you who has said: "Where sin increased, grace abounded all the more" (Romans 5:20b). Then, your fasting, mourning and weeping will be over, for God is always ready "to console those who [weep and] mourn [and fast], to give them beauty for ashes, the oil of joy for mourning, the garment of praise for the spirit of heaviness; that they may be called trees of righteousness, the planting of the LORD, that He may be glorified" (Isaiah 61:3). Scripture says that "oil and perfume delight the heart" (Proverbs 27:9). How much more God's holy oil of gladness (cf. Psalm 23:5b; 45:8b; 89:21), which is able to take away from your souls the burden and yoke of your sins (cf. Isaiah 10:27), will make you glad in the LORD, when you will "taste and see that the LORD is good" (Psalm 34:9a).

Be attentive to the exhortation of Saint Paul the Apostle: "Now it is high time to awake out of sleep; for now our salvation is nearer than when [you] first believed. The night is far spent, the day is at hand. Therefore, [...] cast off the works of darkness, and [...] put on the armor of light. [...] Walk properly as in the day" (Romans 13:11–13). Awake out of the sleep of your spiritual death, and cast off the evil works of darkness which darken your priestly souls, then you will walk properly as in the day, not as in the night; then you will walk in the light of Life and Truth. "For everyone practicing evil hates the light and does not come to the light, lest his deeds should be exposed. But he who does the truth comes to the light, that his deeds may be clearly seen, that they have been done in God" (John 3:20–21). God cries out through the Prophet Malachi: "You have gone away from My ordinances and have not kept them. Return to Me, and I will return to you" (Malachi 3:7a.b). As Tobit says in his prayer: "When you turn back to [God] with all your heart to do what is right before Him, then He will turn back to you, and no longer hide His face from you. [...] Turn back, you sinners! Do the right before Him; perhaps He may look with favor upon you and show you mercy" (Tobit 13:6a.e).

At the time of the Old Testament, God called Moses and Aaron to be the spiritual leaders of Israel, but they failed. Therefore, the LORD said to Moses and Aaron: "Because you did not trust in Me, to show My Holiness before the eyes of the Israelites, therefore you shall not bring this assembly into the land that I have given them" (Numbers 20:12). Moses and Aaron did not enter the promised land due to their unfaithfulness. And so, beware all of you who are appointed as shepherds in the Roman-Catholic Church to lead the People of God, lest you yourselves be rejected (cf. 1 Corinthians 9:27). Do not take your salvation for granted, but learn the fear of the LORD which will protect you against the crime of the profanation of the Eucharist, and will be the very first step on your journey back to Jesus Christ. Do not even try to hide your terrible sins committed against the Living and Life-giving Eucharistic Jesus; rather, listen to the Wisdom of God who admonishes you, on the pages of Sacred Scripture, in the following words: "He who conceals his sins will not prosper, but whoever confesses and forsakes them will obtain mercy" (Proverbs 28:13; cf. 1 John 1:9). So then, "'return, O rebellious children,' says the LORD; 'for I am married to you'" (Jeremiah 3:14a.b.c). "'For I know the thoughts that I think toward you,' says the LORD, 'thoughts of peace and not of evil, to give you a future and a hope. Then you will call upon Me and go and pray to Me, and I will listen to you. And you will seek Me and find Me, when you search for Me with all your heart. I will be found by you,' says the LORD, 'and I will bring you back from your [spiritual] captivity'" (Jeremiah 29:11–14a) into which you have fallen by incurring excommunication for your profanation of the Eucharist, when you desecrated the Atoning, Redemptive, Salvific Blood of Christ by pouring it into the sacrarium. Therefore, ask the Apostolic See for an absolution, because you live in the state of permanent excommunication;

then, confess your sins with a sincere and profound regret; finally, abandon your sins through your total conversion. Avoid your eternal condemnation for being stiff-necked people, and do not postpone your reconciliation with your LORD, but find yourselves in Him again, because "there is now no condemnation for those who are in Christ Jesus" (Romans 8:1). Return, then, to the LORD by hiding and sheltering yourselves in His Life-giving wounds which so many times you opened by your lack of faith and of love. Fall with your faces to the feet of Jesus Christ and pay Him homage (cf. Matthew 2:11a); wash His bleeding wounds with your regretful, sorrowful, remorseful tears of repentance, for He first wept over you (cf. Matthew 23:37–39; Luke 13:34–35; John 11:35); kiss His loving wounds with your profound love, for "by His wounds we are healed" (Isaiah 53:5b); imitate the Good Samaritan, and pour on the suffering wounds of Jesus a soothing oil of your tenderness, as well as a hospitable and restorative wine of your reparation, solicitude and solace; finally, bandage His forgiving wounds (cf. Luke 10:34a) with your "humbled and contrite heart" (Psalm 51:19b) and with your fidelity. Be like the Biblical sinful woman who washed Jesus' "feet with her tears, and wiped them with the hair of her head; and she kissed His feet and anointed them with the fragrant oil" (Luke 7:38). How much more should you prostrate yourselves with sincere grief before our LORD, clinging to His feet and anointing them with a very precious oil, produced by your hearts, and the Mother Church would be filled with the fragrant oil of your profound conversion (cf. John 12:3b).

Listen! Do not waste your time, and do not gamble with the salvation of your souls so lavishly bestowed upon you by the Heavenly Father in His Beloved Son Jesus Christ, but "today, if you hear His voice, do not harden your hearts..." (Psalm 95:7b–8; cf. Hebrews 3:7b.15b; 4:7b). "Do not be deceived, God cannot be mocked" (Galatians 6:7a). Therefore, He calls you to an authentic and total conversion, saying: "Break off your sins by being righteous" (Daniel 4:24b). "Repent, and turn from all your transgressions, so that iniquity will not be your ruin. Cast away from you all the transgressions which you have committed, and get yourselves a new heart and a new spirit" (Ezekiel 18:30c.31a). "Submit to God. Resist the devil and he will flee from you. Draw near to God and He will draw near to you. Cleanse your hands, you sinners; and purify your hearts, you double-minded. Lament and mourn and weep! Let your laughter be turned to mourning and your joy to gloom. Humble yourselves in the sight of the LORD, and He will lift you up" (James 4:7–10). "Turn now from your evil ways and your evil deeds" (Zechariah 1:4c). "Return to Me, and I will return to you" (Malachi 3:7b; cf. Zechariah 1:3c). "Turn to Me with all your heart, with fasting, with weeping, and with mourning. Rend your heart, and not your garments; return to the LORD, your God, for He is gracious and merciful, slow to anger, and of great kindness; and He relents from doing harm. Who knows whether He will not turn and relent, and leave a blessing behind Him, a grain offering and a drink offering for the LORD, your God?" (Joel 2:12–14). Yes, may the Merciful God incline your minds and hearts to accept and to cherish with your profound faith and genuine love the Most Holy Grain Offering of the Eucharistic Bread and the Most Holy Drink Offering of the Eucharistic Wine; then, indeed, the Eucharistic Blessing of our LORD Jesus Christ will rest upon you. But first you need to come to your senses (cf. Luke 15:17a), and each of you must humiliate himself, heartily confessing: "I have sinned against the LORD" (2 Samuel 12:13b; cf. Luke 15:18b.21b); "all the day my disgrace is before me, and the shame of my face has covered me" (Psalm 44:16); "therefore, I abhor myself, and repent in dust and ashes" (Job 42:6).

"Out of much affliction and anguish of heart I wrote [this book], with many tears" (2 Corinthians 2:4), confident "that I might by all means save some" (1 Corinthians 9:22b). And "if I made you sorry with my [book], I do not regret it" (2 Corinthians 7:8a), hoping "that your sorrow [will lead you] to repentance, [that] you [will be] made sorry in a Godly manner" (2 Corinthians 7:9). "For Godly sorrow produces repentance leading to salvation, not to be regretted; but the sorrow of the world produces death" (2 Corinthians 7:10). It is better for you to enter Heaven with Godly sorrow than to go down to hell with demonic pride and hardness of heart.

In my closing statement, addressed to you, priests, who so brutally profane the Most Holy and the Most Precious Blood of our LORD Jesus Christ, I want to make it very clear that I personally do not judge nor condemn *you*, but I do judge and I do condemn *your evil deeds*. However, if you do not convert, the words of this book will judge and condemn not only *your evil deeds*, but also *you yourselves* on the Day of the Last Judgment. Therefore, convert now and begin a new life in Jesus the Christ!

3.

An Appeal to All Catholics of Good Will for Protection of the Sacrament of the Eucharist

*H*aving presented the huge problem of the profanation of the Most Precious Blood of our LORD, which is widespread in North America as a pestilence, I want simultaneously to appeal to all Catholics, who have faith in and love for the Eucharistic Jesus, to resist this evil practice.

What drives me on, in writing the present book, is my compelling desire to inform as many Catholics as possible about this horrible crime, in the very bosom of the Roman-Catholic Church, which is to the great spiritual detriment of the People of God, and especially to the detriment of innocent children: the altar-boys and altar-girls, who have access to the sacristy where the Most Holy Blood of Christ is usually being profaned. Therefore, I am asking you, on my knees, Brothers and Sisters in our LORD Jesus Christ, to join me and to become an active part in our common campaign against the devastating evil of the profanation of the

Most Holy Eucharist. Please, help our Holy Mother Church to overcome this unspeakable abuse which consumes the souls of so many Catholics; please, help to turn their lives around as soon as possible so that they avoid eternal punishment. And let us not be sluggish, but let us spur ourselves on in our struggle against this barbaric crime. Please, bear always in mind that we sin not only when we do something wrong, but also when we fail to do what is right, because as Saint James the Apostle writes in his letter: "Anyone [...] who knows the good he ought to do and does not do it, commits sin" (James 4:17). And he goes on, saying: "If anyone among you wanders from the truth, and someone turns him back, let him know that he who turns a sinner from the error of his way will save a soul from death and cover a multitude of sins" (James 5:19–20). God has promised through the Prophet Ezekiel that "if a wicked man turns from all his sins which he has committed, keeps all My statutes, and does what is lawful and right, he shall surely live; he shall not die. None of the transgressions which he has committed shall be remembered against him; because of the righteousness which he has done, he shall live. Do I have any pleasure at all that the wicked should die, [...] and not that he should turn from his ways and live?" (Ezekiel 18:21–23). The Psalmist also says: "Blessed is he whose transgression is forgiven, whose sin is covered. Blessed is the man to whom the LORD does not impute iniquity, and in whose spirit there is no deceit" (Psalm 32:1–2). Therefore, please, do not sin by being co-responsible for the desecration of the Eucharist through your *fruitless silence*, but feel you are called to offer your *fruitful resistance* against this "liturgical butchery." "For if we sin willfully after we have received the knowledge of the truth, there no longer remains a sacrifice for sins, but a certain fearful expectation of judgment, and fiery indignation which will devour the adversaries" (Hebrews 10:26–27) who have "insulted the Spirit of Grace" (Hebrews 10:29).

"Now the Spirit expressly says that in latter times some will depart from the faith, giving heed to deceiving spirits and doctrines of demons" (1 Timothy 4:1). This time is present now in the lives of all those wicked priests "who have strayed concerning the truth" (2 Timothy 2:18) and who "have strayed concerning the faith" (1 Timothy 6:21a). Because they have not followed the truth about the Eucharist, as it is being taught by the Catholic Church, and because they have lost their faith in the Eucharist, they have desecrated the Most Sacred Blood of our LORD Jesus Christ. Only those who give heed to deceiving spirits are able to do it. All these obstinate priests "resist the truth: men of corrupt minds, disapproved concerning the faith" (2 Timothy 3:8).

My Beloved, since you already know this, "be on your guard lest, being led astray by the error of lawless men, you also fall from your own steadfastness" (2 Peter 3:17). Our Divine Master teaches in His Gospel: "That servant who knew his master's will, and did not prepare himself or do according to his will, shall be beaten with many lashes" (Luke 12:47). "Let us lay aside every weight, and the sin which so easily ensnares us, and let us run with endurance the race that is set before us, looking unto Jesus, the author and finisher of our faith, who for the joy that was set before Him endured the cross, despising the shame, and has sat down at the right hand of the throne of God" (Hebrews 12:1–2). "Therefore, I urge you, Brothers [and Sisters], by the Mercies of God to offer your bodies as a living sacrifice, holy and acceptable to God, your rational worship. And do not be conformed to this world, but be transformed by the renewal of your mind, so that you may judge what is the will of God, what is good, pleasing and perfect" (Romans 12:1–2). "Do not grow slack, but be fervent in Spirit; He whom you serve is the LORD" (Romans 12:11). Do not yield even an inch in defending the Eucharistic Jesus, and in the face of many hardships, trials and even insults, which may sometimes come your way, remain unshaken, having the LORD as your Rock. Side always with God, not with those who act against God, and never dread the people, but always trust in God (cf. Psalm 56:5.12), "for you have not received a spirit of slavery, leading you back into fear ..." (Romans 8:15a). And so, do not be enslaved by being afraid of people, but step up and speak up. Do not be silent, speechless and indifferent onlookers, when Jesus Christ is being treated so brutally by the servants of His Altar, but be vocal advocates of the truth and courageous doers of what is right by obeying the voice of our LORD which resounds in the voice of His Holy Church. Do NOT obey those priests who try to force you to desecrate the Eucharist. Many associate pastors, deacons and extraordinary Eucharistic ministers profane the Most Holy Blood of Christ under cover of their wrongly understood obedience to their pastors, but this is a false perception of obedience. We obey our superiors, but with the stipulation that, in their decisions, they do not violate the fundamental principles of faith and morals. However, if your pastor acts contrary to Canon Law and orders you to profane the Eucharist, then – in this particular case – you must NOT obey him. Do not be so blindly "obedient" to your local superior that you disobey the Holy Father and act against God Himself. Do not be like a younger son in a family for whom the authority of his older brother is more important than the authority of their father. Your obedience must always serve all that is morally good, not that which is morally evil. Do not be so subserviently "obedient" to your local pastor that you forfeit your soul to hell. If your pastor forces you to do anything which stands in strong opposition to what is officially taught by the Holy Father and the Apostolic See, you must always choose the way of the Roman-Catholic Church, not your superior. Listen to your Supreme Shepherd Jesus Christ who is acting in the heart of His Church through the Holy Father and the Magisterium of the Church in accordance with what our LORD has said to the Apostles: "He who hears you hears Me, he who rejects you rejects Me, and he who rejects Me rejects Him who sent Me" (Luke 10:16). Here, Jesus Christ identifies Himself totally with His disciples, and this is also true today; Jesus is not standing beside the Church, but He is acting *within* the Church through the Holy Father and bishops united with him in one and undivided teaching. Therefore, as regards the fundamental truths of faith and morals, as well as the fundamental liturgical practices, concerning the Eucharist, the voice of the Magisterium of the Church is the voice of Jesus Christ Himself. Do not listen to the jabber of a false pastor, but attend to the sound of the clear voice of the Roman-Catholic Church. Do not be more sensitive to a depraved pastor than to the LORD Himself. It is Jesus Christ who died for you, not your pastor; it is Jesus Christ who has saved you, not your pastor; it is Jesus Christ who will raise you from the dead, not your pastor. So then, sacrifice yourselves to your LORD who leads you to Life, not to a wicked pastor who leads you to death. Be not blindly "obedient" to a corrupt superior, but listen to the voice of the LORD, who speaks through the Holy Father and through the institutions of the Apostolic See, and you will not go astray. Do not follow the sick, perverse and rebellious conscience of an individual superior, lest you be led to insanity, but follow the collective conscience of the Holy Mother Church, and you will live in harmony and peace with God and with those who have His mind. If you follow a deceiver, you will reap a harvest of death, but if you follow the

Church, you will reap a harvest of Life, Life Eternal. So then, relinquish the evil practices of your pastors and their stubborn conduct, and firmly and steadfastly resist them. Note this first of all that Judas was one of the Twelve Apostles, who formed the closest circle of Jesus' disciples, yet nobody followed Judas, and we know how his life ended. Therefore, be vigilant and follow only those priests who follow the law of the Church; do not enter the path of death, but always walk on the path of Life; be the messengers of the Truth preached by Jesus Christ and by His Holy Church. Then the words of the Prophet Isaiah will be fulfilled in you, who cried out, saying: "How beautiful upon the mountains are the feet of him who brings good news, who proclaims peace, who brings glad tidings of good things, who proclaims salvation, who says to Zion, 'Your God reigns'" (Isaiah 52:7). These words can be paraphrased in the following manner: "How beautiful are the feet of those who, following the example of the Good Samaritan, hasten to help the suffering Jesus Christ, so brutally treated through the desecration of the Eucharist; how beautiful are the feet of those who have the courage to admonish those who abuse the Eucharist; how beautiful and how blessed are the feet of those who never cease to manifest their faith and to pray for the conversion of those who incurred an excommunication due to their profanation of the Eucharist." Therefore, do not pay only lip service to your faith in the real presence of Jesus Christ in the Eucharist, but defend Him present in this Most Blessed Sacrament, because, as the Apostle James teaches us: "A man is justified by works, and not by faith only. [...] For just as the body without the spirit is dead, so also faith without works is dead" (James 2:24.26). And Jesus Christ warns us, saying: "Not everyone who says to Me, 'Lord, Lord,' shall enter the kingdom of heaven, but he who does the will of My Father in heaven" (Matthew 7:21);

"Why do you call Me 'LORD, LORD,' and do not do what I tell you?" (Luke 6:46). This is a particular reference to all of us: bishops, priests, deacons and laity. Let us, then, defend our LORD in the Most Holy Eucharist, for He has first defended us against the devil, and has opened for us the gates of Heaven through His Most Precious Wounds. Therefore, do not only complain about the profanation of the Eucharist and do not only mourn over Jesus, badly being treated by His priests, but do something for Him. First of all, please, take action and fight in defense of our LORD, since, in the eyes of God, not onlookers, but doers are justified. Say categorically: "NO" to all those priests who so barbarically treat our LORD Jesus Christ whom He Himself has chosen and sent to show His Holiness before His people (cf. Numbers 20:12). Instead, they act against Him and scandalize the faithful when they desecrate His Most Sacred Blood. They are rebels who "have taught their tongue to speak lies; they weary themselves to commit iniquity" (Jeremiah 9:4b.c). God is "on their lips, but far from their hearts" (Jeremiah 12:2c). They "draw near with their mouths and honor [God] with their lips, but have removed their hearts far from [Him] ... " (Isaiah 29:13b). This is why their thoughts are not the thoughts of God, nor are their ways His ways (cf. Isaiah 55:8a). As false shepherds, they deceive the People of God, and do not speak the truth (cf. Jeremiah 9:4a). Therefore, "Do not believe them, even though they speak smooth words to you" (Jeremiah 12:6c).

The sin of those who demonically profane the Most Holy Eucharist with full awareness and free will is greater than that of Cain and Judas, because both Cain and Judas were seized with remorse after committing their crimes (cf. Genesis 4:13–15; Matthew 27:3–4). Judas admitted to his crime, and he confessed his sin publicly, saying: "I have sinned by betraying Innocent Blood" (Matthew 27:4a). Those, however, who rebelliously act against the Living and Life-giving Eucharistic Jesus do not regret their evil and death-bringing crime. Therefore, they surely belong to the band of Annas, Caiaphas, all the chief priests, the elders of the people, the scribes, the Sanhedrin and the whole multitude of those who crucify Jesus Christ today, whenever they desecrate His Most Holy Blood. As a matter of fact, those who crucify our LORD today, by this criminal practice, are even worse than those who crucified the *historical* Jesus, because those who demanded from Pilate a death sentence for Jesus did not know what they were doing, and we know this from our LORD Himself who, from the height of the cross, prayed to His Heavenly Father, saying: "Father, forgive them, for they do not know what they are doing" (Luke 23:34). And referring to this tragic blindness of the executioners of Jesus Christ, the Apostle Paul writes to the Corinthians as follows: "We speak the wisdom of God in a mystery, the hidden wisdom which God ordained before the ages for our glory, which none of the rulers of this age knew, for if they had known it, they would not have crucified the LORD of Glory" (1 Corinthians 2:7–8). Their ignorance was forgiven by Jesus Christ, but what kind of excuse can be found for those who crucify the Eucharistic Jesus today after two thousand years of knowledge, experience and teaching of the Church about the Eucharist? All priests are morally obligated to know *ex professo* the Mystery of the Most Holy Eucharist and the juridical regulations pertaining to this Most August Sacrament. If anyone wants to be a pilot, he must know how to take off, how to fly and how to land, otherwise, after his first attempt, he would need somebody to carry him off to a place of rest. It is taken for granted that every driver knows that he must stop at a stop-sign, otherwise, he will be fined by a policeman, and if he caused an accident, nobody would accept his excuse that he did not know this road-rule. Likewise, no priest can make any excuse by saying that he did not know that the left-over Eucharistic Blood of Christ must not be poured into the sacrarium. A priest who does not know so fundamental a regulation should not be admitted to the altar; this is liturgical barbarism; this is liturgical butchery; this is liturgical abortion done to our LORD. Is this the way we are to re-pay Jesus Christ for His Great Love towards us, making Himself perpetually present in the Most Holy Eucharist?

Pouring the Most Sacred Blood of Christ into the sacrarium, the rebellious and unfaithful priests crucify our LORD over and over again, and they also want the People of God to "run with them in the same flood of [evil]" (1 Peter 4:4), when they encourage them to profane the Most Holy Eucharist. But you "do not be yoked together with unbelievers. For what fellowship has righteousness with lawlessness? And what communion has light with darkness?" (2 Corinthians 6:14). As the faithful disciples of Jesus Christ, you are to "shine as lights in the world" (Philippians 2:15) with the Light of our Divine Master who has said: "I am the Light of the world. He who follows Me will not walk in darkness, but will have the Light of Life" (John 8:12b). "Walk while you have the Light, lest darkness overtake you; he who walks in darkness does not know where he is going. While you have the Light, believe in the Light, that you may become sons [and daughters] of Light" (John 12:35c–36a; cf. 1 John 2:11) that so lovingly shines in the Blessed Sacrament of the Eucharist.

Therefore, do not abandon our LORD, the Light of the world, but walk in His Light by your fidelity to Him. You know how He was alone in the Garden of Olives, and how He was forsaken by His Apostles at the hour when He was arrested, and then at His trials before the high priests and

Pilate, and when He was scourged at a pillar, crowned with thorns, and when He was carrying His cross, and was crucified, and finally when He was dying on the cross in terrible agony for three hours. Do not be indifferent to the fact that your LORD is being treated so brutally today by those who should be first in standing at the foot of His cross. When Jesus was dying on the cross, He prayed to His Father with the words of Psalm 22: "My God, My God, why have You forsaken Me?" (Matthew 27:46b; Mark 15:34b; Psalm 22:2a). And today, when His Most Precious Blood is being poured into the sacrarium, He is complaining to His Father over and over again with the words of the same Psalm 22, saying: "Many bulls have surrounded Me [...]. They open wide their mouths at Me, like a ravening and roaring lion. I am poured out like water, and all My bones are out of joint [...]. You have brought Me to the dust of death. For dogs have surrounded Me; the congregation of the wicked has enclosed Me. They pierced My hands and My feet [...]. But You, O LORD, do not be far from Me; O My Strength, hasten to help Me! Deliver Me from the sword, My precious life from the power of the dog. Save Me from the lion's mouth, and from the horns of the wild oxen!" (Psalm 22:13a.14–15a.16b–17.20–22a). Jesus Christ has given Himself in the Eucharist into our hands, as the Innocent Lamb of God, with confidence that we will treat Him with faith and reverence, but He is being betrayed and rejected by His own (cf. John 1:11). Therefore, today He cries out to all of us who love Him: "Rescue Me from the sword of the wicked, from the power of the dogs who shed My Blood; save Me from the lions' mouths, and from the horns of the wild oxen who tear My Body." Let us, then, defend our Eucharistic LORD from being so brutally treated by unfaithful priests. Let us resist all those who prowl in the bosom of the Roman-Catholic Church as dogs, lions and wild oxen, crucifying Jesus over and over again. Let us stop this liturgical massacre; let us finally stop this demonic butchery.

Look at the Parable about the Good Samaritan and notice that those who were not moved with pity at the sight of the man beaten by robbers were a priest and a Levite (cf. Luke 10:30–32). Those who belonged to the priestly clan in Israel showed their indifference, but a Samaritan fulfilled what the priests should have done. The story of the Good Samaritan is relevant to us even today. It is the priests, first of all, who are to cherish the Eucharistic Jesus Christ, but they abandon Him as do the Biblical priest and Levite, and He is treated even worse, because His priests put Him into the ground. In face of so great an indifference of so many priests, be like the Biblical Good Samaritan, and do not be discouraged by the negligence of priests, but take care of your LORD who suffers so much by their hands. Therefore, when you know that a profanation of the Eucharist is taking place in your parish, please, do not desert the wounded Jesus, and do not imitate the behavior of the priest and the Levite in the Parable of the Good Samaritan. They left a man who, going down from Jerusalem to Jericho, fell among evil people who stripped him of his clothing, wounded him, and departed, leaving him half dead (cf. Luke 10:30–32). This is exactly what happens to our LORD when He is thrown away into the sacrarium and into the ground. Therefore, be moved with pity for Jesus, suffering injuries done by His own people; He is coming over and over again to His own in the Most Holy Eucharist, yet He is being rejected over and over again by His own priests. In the Parable of the Good Samaritan, Jesus Christ tells us how a certain Samaritan had compassion on a bleeding and dying man (cf. Luke 10:33). "He went to him and bandaged his wounds, pouring on oil and wine; and he set him on his own animal, brought him to an inn, and took care of him" (Luke 10:34). Therefore, imitate the attitude of the Good Samaritan, and do not abandon our wounded and suffering LORD, but set Him on the shoulders of your unshaken faith, bring Him into the inn of your heart and take care of Him by the way you proclaim and defend Him present in the Most Holy Eucharist. Do not leave your LORD alone, for He did not leave you alone when you lived in the bondage of the devil, but He came to seek you. He found you and saved you. "Receive Him with open, outstretched hands, for it was on His own hands that He sketched you. Receive Him who laid your foundations on the palms of His hands. Receive Him, for He took upon Himself all that belongs to us except sin, to consume what is ours in what is His."[107] The Son of God has become the Son of Man so as we might become the adopted children of God. He has become like us, "yet without sin" (Hebrews 4:15), in order to restore in us the perfect image and likeness of God which we had lost through our sin. We would have suffered eternal death, had Jesus not suffered in time. Never would we have been freed from sinful flesh, had Christ not taken on Himself the weight of our sinful flesh. We would have suffered everlasting unhappiness, had it not been for His Eternal Mercy. We would never have returned to life, had He not accepted death on our behalf. We would have been lost, if He had not hastened to our aid. We would have perished, had He not died for us on the Altar of the Cross.[108] Therefore, let us be as the Most Blessed Mother of Jesus Christ, Saint John the Evangelist and the women who followed our LORD even to His cross, then we will be first to see and hear the voice of the Risen LORD. Let us be sure that whenever

---

[107] "From a discourse by Saint Andrew of Crete, bishop," [in]: *The Liturgy of the Hours, vol. IV* (New York 1975), p. 546.

[108] Cf. "From a sermon by Saint Augustine, bishop," [in]: *The Liturgy of the Hours, vol. I* (New York 1975), p. 379.

we combat the profanation of the Eucharist, the LORD is *always* with us. And so, do not be discouraged by the ridiculous theories, opinions and interpretations of those who try to defend their evil practice of the profanation of the Eucharist, because what they do is pure insanity. Do not listen to them, but attend to the voice of the Church whose documents pertaining to the profanation of the Eucharist are unequivocal; this is an issue which is not negotiable. Keep in mind that it is impossible for faithful Catholics to elude problems; this is possible only for lukewarm Catholics, but our LORD says to them in the Book of Revelation: "I know your works that you are neither cold nor hot. I wish that you were either cold or hot. So then, because you are lukewarm, and neither cold nor hot, I will vomit you out of My mouth" (Revelation 3:15–16). And Jesus Christ teaches us in the Gospel of Saint Matthew, saying: "Let your 'Yes' be 'Yes,' and your 'No,' 'No.' For whatever is more than these is from the evil one" (Matthew 5:37). This is how we Christians are to proclaim the Good News of our LORD. According to the Teaching of our Divine Master, there is no common ground between "yes" and "no," between truth and error, and it is impossible to be simultaneously cold and hot. God is absolutely perfect; therefore, with God everything is and it must be perfectly univocal, explicit, unequivocal, inasmuch as any kind of ambiguity would be against God's perfection. In other words, with God there exists nothing between *white* and *black*, but everything must be either *white* or *black*. In short, the color gray does not belong to the "Divine coloration," because gray color stands for what is vague, indistinct, indeterminate, and this, in turn, has nothing in common with God's perfection. Gray color is preferred by liberal and heretical priests, by the intellectual, spiritual and moral color-blind persons; gray color is typical of miserable thinkers who confuse many Catholics by creating in them a "gray" Catholicism which leads them nowhere. Clarity both in teaching and in pastoral service is absolutely fundamental, and this clarity is possible when it is enlivened and imbued with the spirit of faith. It was not only a lack of sound doctrine and of solid pastoral leadership, but also a lack of faith which has led many Catholics to the crime of the profanation of the Eucharist.

The Apostle Paul teaches us that "since we have the same spirit of faith, according to what is written: 'I believed and therefore I spoke' (Psalm 116:10a), we also believe and therefore speak" (2 Corinthians 4:13). Thus, our faith enables us, and urges us to speak out in defense of Jesus Christ, who has first spoken on our behalf by shedding His own Blood for our Salvation, the Most Holy Blood of the New Covenant "that speaks better than that of Abel" (Hebrews 12:24). So then, put yourselves at the service of the very noble task of giving your loving hearts to our Eucharistic LORD by resisting actively the profanation of Holy Communion. Set Jesus Christ above everyone and above everything, and never be intimidated by arrogant and abusive priests who will ridicule your fidelity to and your zeal for the Eucharistic LORD whom you will defend, opposing the profanation of the Most Holy Communion.

Now, how should you act in this situation? The answer is very simply: Follow the instruction of our LORD Jesus Christ who has said: "If your brother sins against you, go and tell him his fault between you and him alone. If he hears you, you have gained your brother. But if he will not hear, take with you one or two more, that 'by the mouth of two or three witnesses every word may be established' (Deuteronomy 19:15). And if he refuses to hear them, tell it to the Church. But if he refuses even to hear the Church, let him be to you like a pagan and a tax collector" (Matthew 18:15–17; cf.

Ezekiel 18:21–23). So then, first talk personally with your pastors, deacons and extraordinary Eucharistic ministers about this terrible abuse. If they do not listen to the voice of the Church, then contact your bishop, but if even he is negligent, then write letters to the Holy Father. In short, never give up! Bind yourselves, with an uncompromising, relentless and unceasing determination, to defend our LORD present in the Most Holy Eucharist. As Christians you belong to Jesus Christ who has laid down His Life for your Salvation. "[He] gave [His] back to those who struck [Him], and [His] cheeks to those who plucked out [His] beard; [He] did not hide [His] face from buffets and spitting" (Isaiah 50:6). Therefore, sacrifice, in turn, your life for your LORD, fighting against the profanation of the Eucharist. This is a task of every individual Christian who loyally adheres to the teaching and the law of the Roman–Catholic Church. And let me express this task in the following figurative terms: "Christian, do not hide your head in the sand, because you are not an ostrich, but stretch out your neck, since you are a lamb in Jesus Christ, the Lamb of God." "For God has not given us a spirit of fear, but of power and of love and of a sound mind" (2 Timothy 1:7). Remember that you belong to "the Church militant,"[109] as it has been stated by the Council of Basel at Session 2, held on February 15, 1432, and by the Fifth Lateran Council at Session 11 held on December 19, 1516. Indeed, the Church of Christ is militant *spiritually*, and this is one of its vital features. And because the Church, to which we belong, is militant *spiritually*, therefore, the weapons of our militancy are not arms, but our faith, prayer, fortitude, personal sacrifice and concrete actions inspired by the Gospel, our *Divine* weapon, called by Saint Paul the Apostle: "The sword of the Spirit which is the word of God" (Ephesians 6:17). However,

---

[109] N. P. Tanner, *vol. I*, op. cit., pp. 456.635.

the Church must courageously and manfully manifest its struggle, first of all, in fighting against the errors in its very bosom which are far more dangerous for the Church than its outer enemies. The *external* enemies *unite* the Church and make it even stronger, whereas the *internal* enemies *divide* the Church and make it ever weaker. As our LORD teaches us: "Every kingdom divided against itself is brought to desolation, and every city or house divided against itself will not stand" (Matthew 12:25b; cf. Mark 3:24–25; Luke 11:17b). The profanation of the Eucharist has divided the House of God and has seriously wounded the Mystical Body of the Church in its innermost essence. Therefore, Brothers and Sisters, be vigilant, be alert and resist this diabolical practice, steadfast in your faith (cf. 1 Peter 5:8–9). Please, do not be like sleeping infants or as the people who walk in the darkness of cowardice, inasmuch as you have been called to be "light in the LORD. Walk as children of light for the fruit of the Spirit is in all goodness, righteousness, and truth, finding out what is acceptable to the LORD. And have no fellowship with the unfruitful works of darkness, but rather expose them" (Ephesians 5:8–11). Indeed, the profanation of the Most Holy Eucharist belongs, beyond any reasonable doubt, to the unfruitful works of darkness, and it is clearly the most grave abuse which we must NOT conceal or hide from the public, but we must expose this criminal activity; we must bring it into light, because the Sacrament of the Most Holy Eucharist is not a private issue, but public in the fullest sense of the word.

Thousands of people know about the problem of the profanation of the Eucharist, but they do not have any juridical power to stop this barbaric butchery. However, even those who have no juridical power can still use the power of their faith, if they possess it, and which can serve to persuade and convert the abusers of the Eucharist. Therefore, I am appealing to all of you priests, deacons and extraordinary Eucharistic ministers: Never *actively* nor *passively* consent to the profanation of the Most Holy Communion; never concur in this merciless act of crucifying our Eucharistic LORD Jesus Christ over and over again when your superiors try to force you to do it, and do not keep silent, but show your Christian character. Remember, your passive silence will also give consent to this evil practice. Say categorically: "NO" to the profanation of the Eucharist in word and deed, and do not go along with those who have lost their faith. Save yourselves from this corrupt generation of the profaners of the Eucharist (cf. Acts 2:40b). Many of them can ridicule you, using their authority, but "fear not, Beloved, you are safe; take courage and be strong" (Daniel 10:19b), and "rejoice to the extent that you partake of Christ's sufferings, that when His Glory is revealed, you may also be glad with exceeding joy. If you are reproached for the Name of Christ, blessed are you, for the Spirit of Glory and of God rests upon you. On their part, He is blasphemed, but on your part, He is glorified" (1 Peter 4:13–14). So then, the one who wants to have his share in the future Glory of the LORD must now partake of His sufferings. That's how we really prove and confirm that we love Him. Saint Sister Maria Faustina Kowalska writes in her "Diary" that "the quintessence of love is sacrifice and suffering. Truth wears a crown of thorns. Prayer involves the intellect, the will and the emotions."[110] I can well imagine how much you will suffer by resisting all those obstinate, rebellious priests who desecrate the Eucharist who "have cast off their first faith" (1 Timothy 5:12). "But if anyone does not provide for his own, and especially for those of [the Household of God], he has denied the faith and is worse than an unbeliever" (1 Timothy

---

[110] Saint Maria Faustina Kowalska, *Diary* (Stockbridge, Massachusetts 2003), p. 410.

5:8). Therefore, please, do NOT follow them! If you are an extraordinary Eucharistic minister, and your pastor tries to force you to pour the Most Holy Blood of Christ into the sacrarium, NEVER accede to it. You must not ever on any grounds follow this evil practice which is undoubtedly demonic. Sacred Scripture exhorts us: "Ponder the path of your feet, and let all your ways be established. Do not turn aside to the right or to the left; remove your foot from evil" (Proverbs 4:26–27; cf. Deuteronomy 5:32b). It is better for you to quit as a minister of the Eucharist than to incur an excommunication and to be an occasion of sin to others who, seeing you pour the Most Sacred Blood of Christ into the sacrarium, would be scandalized. The Most Holy Sacrament of the Eucharist requires the most holy service. Therefore, if you know about the profanation of Holy Communion in your diocese, please, apprise your bishop immediately of that abuse. Never side with those who profane the Eucharist; never consent to this crime, then on the Day of the Last Judgment Jesus Christ will say to you: "'Come, you blessed of My Father, inherit the Kingdom prepared for you from the foundation of the world' (Matthew 25:34b); for I was rejected by the servants of My Altar, and you accepted Me with love; I was disregarded by them, and you had regard for Me; I was dishonored, and you honored Me; I was forgotten, and you remembered Me; I was disbelieved, and you believed in Me; I was profaned, and you adored Me; I was abandoned, and you opened the doors of your hearts and welcomed Me; I was not loved, and You loved Me sincerely and fervently. Therefore, I now 'open to [you] the gates of righteousness; [...] go through them, and [...] praise the LORD. This is the gate of the LORD, through which the righteous may enter' (Psalm 118:19–20)."

So then, take heart, be courageous and never give up fighting for our LORD Jesus Christ present in the Sacrament of the Most Holy Communion. I know that those priests who profane the Eucharist can be very rude to you, as they were to me, but what else should you expect from unfaithful, rebellious and arrogant priests. Jesus Christ Himself said to His Apostles: "Remember the word that I said to you, 'A servant is not greater than his master.' If they persecuted Me, they will also persecute you" (John 15:20a.b.c). And look! It was priests who so unjustly judged the *historical* Jesus and demanded His death on a cross at the hands of Pilate, and now, it is priests again who crucify the *Eucharistic* Jesus with their own hands. The priests of the Old Covenant did not know what they were doing (cf. Luke 23:34; 1 Corinthians 2:8b). However, the priests of the New Covenant know what they are doing; they know whom they are crucifying over and over again; therefore, they are surely worse than those priests who rejected and crucified the *historical* Jesus.

Our Divine Master said to His disciples: "You are My friends if you do whatever I command you. No longer do I call you servants, for a servant does not know what his master is doing; but I have called you friends, for all things that I heard from My Father I have made known to you" (John 15:14–15). Likewise, all the priests who are chosen by Jesus Christ are His friends, but only if they fulfill His Divine Will. They are called "to shepherd the Church of God that [Jesus Christ] purchased with His own Blood" (Acts 20:28), to build up His Precious and Beloved Household, that we are (cf. Hebrews 3:6), but they tear it asunder, being "a brood of evildoers, children who are corrupters" (Isaiah 1:4a), who make of the House of God "a den of thieves" (Matthew 21:13b; Mark 11:17b; Luke 19:46b; John 2:16b; cf. Isaiah 56:7; Jeremiah 7,11). The priests who desecrate the Eucharist and mislead others are those negligent shepherds who do "not care for those who are cut off, nor seek the young, nor heal those that are broken, nor feed those that still stand" (Zechariah 11:16a; cf. Ezekiel 34:2–6). They crucify Jesus Christ over and over again, and His Most Holy Body is covered with countless wounds inflicted by His own priests. Therefore, our LORD complains through the Prophet Zechariah, saying: "These [are the] wounds [...] with which I was wounded in the house of my friends" (Zechariah 13:6b.d). Surely those priests who profane the Blood of Christ are not His friends, but His traitors. Thus, the words of the Prophet Micah are fulfilled when he says: "A man's enemies are the men of his own household" (Micah 7:6b). This prophecy is also quoted in the Gospel of Saint Matthew by our LORD: "A man's enemies will be those of his own household" (Matthew 10:36). If those evil priests – who are of Christ's own Household, but profane His Most Holy Blood – are the enemies of the LORD, then do not expect, and do not be surprised that they may not be sweet to you, but rather bitter or even nasty. However, God says through the Prophet Isaiah: "Listen to Me, you who know righteousness, you people in whose heart is My Law: Do not fear the reproach of men, nor be afraid of their insults" (Isaiah 51:7). At the time of the Old Testament, God sent the Prophet Ezekiel on a mission, saying: "Son of man, I am sending you to the Israelites, to a nation of rebels who have rebelled against Me; they and their ancestors have revolted against Me to this very day. They are hard of face and obstinate of heart. I am sending you to them, and you shall say to them, 'Thus says the LORD God.' As for them, whether they hear or whether they refuse – for they are a rebellious house – yet they will know that a prophet has been among them. And you, son of man, do not be afraid of them nor be afraid of their words, though briers and thorns are with you and you dwell among scorpions; do not be afraid of their words or dismayed by their looks, though they are a rebellious house. You shall speak My words to them, whether they hear or whether they refuse, for they are rebellious" (Ezekiel 2:3b–7). "The house of Israel will not listen to you, because they will not listen to Me; for all the house of Israel are impudent and hard-hearted. [...] Do not be afraid of them, nor be dismayed at their looks, though they are a rebellious house" (Ezekiel 3:7.9b). And let the encouragement of Saint Paul the Apostle always echo in our minds and hearts who urges us with the following words: "Proclaim the Word; be persistent whether the time is favorable or unfavorable; convince, rebuke, exhort, with all longsuffering and teaching" (2 Timothy 4:2). "And if anyone does not obey [your] word [...], note that person and do not keep company with him, that he may be ashamed. Yet do not count him as an enemy, but admonish him as a brother" (2 Thessalonians 3:14–15; cf. Galatians 6:1). Therefore, do not be discouraged when rebellious priests will not listen to you. There were many, in the past, who did not listen to the Prophets and even to our Divine Master Jesus Christ, and yet He fulfilled the Will of His Heavenly Father perfectly and finished His mission on earth. So then, follow in His foot-steps and be on your way to fight against the profanation of the Eucharist and the ultimate victory will be yours in Jesus Christ our LORD. I know that sometimes those who desecrate the Eucharist can even bring you to tears, but never lose heart, never be discouraged and may these words of the Psalmist resound in your ears: "Those who sow in tears will reap in joy; those who go out weeping, bearing seed for sowing, will return with shouts of joy, carrying their sheaves" (Psalm 126:5–6). "And God will wipe away every tear from their eyes" (Revelation 21:4a). Therefore, may the listless spirit never govern you, but have courage for the present and hope for the future. "And whatever you do, do it heartily, as to the LORD and not to men, knowing that from the LORD you will receive the reward of the inheritance; for you serve the LORD Christ" (Colossians 3:23–24). Bear in mind that if you are willing to share in the sufferings of Christ, you will also share abundantly in His consolation and in His Glory (cf. 2 Corinthians 1:5.7), because, as the Wisdom of God says on the pages of Sacred Scripture: "The fruit of noble struggles is a glorious one" (Wisdom 3:15a). Therefore, do not give allegiance to evil and to the spirit of the rebellious (cf. Ephesians 2:2). Follow the *collective* conscience and faith of the Catholic Church, NOT the *personal* conscience and practices of those who profane the Eucharist and give you their personal, uneducated and insane opinions pertaining to what you should do with the remaining Blood of Jesus Christ. "[Keep] faith and a good conscience, which some have rejected and suffered shipwreck in regard to the faith" (1 Timothy 1:19), and bear in mind that the *personal* teaching of a person is NOT above the *collective* and *universal* Teaching of the Roman-Catholic Church. Be slaves of Jesus Christ, NOT of the false shepherds. Our LORD warns us, saying: "Beware of false prophets, who come to you in sheep's clothing, but inwardly they are ravenous wolves" (Matthew 7:15; cf. Luke 6:43–45). And Saint Peter the Apostle writes in his Second Letter: "There were also false prophets among the people, even as there will be false teachers among you, who will secretly bring in destructive heresies, even denying the LORD who bought them, and bring on themselves swift destruction" (2 Peter 2:1). Those who poured the Most Holy Blood of Christ into the sacrarium, knowing that this practice is strictly prohibited by the Roman-Catholic Church, "adopted an attitude of opposition and, prodigal of their good name and enemies to their own honour, they strove to their utmost with pestilential daring to rend the unity of the Holy Roman and Universal Church and the seamless robe of Christ (cf. John 19:23), and with serpentlike bites to lacerate the womb of the Pious and Holy Mother herself (the Ecumenical Council of Florence at Session 9 held on March 23, 1440;"[111] see also the Fifth Ecumenical Lateran Council at Session 11 held on December 19, 1516).[112] They are mindless of the fact that, through their profanation of the Eucharist, they create chaos in the very bosom of the Roman-Catholic Church, and wound the Mystical Body of Jesus Christ. But you must resist this criminal activity. At the time of the Old Testament, God YHWH said to the People of Israel through Moses: "[You] shall [not] stand by idly when your neighbor's life is at stake" (Leviticus 19:16b). All the more must we defend our Eucharistic LORD who is so cruelly, so ruthlessly being maltreated by so many obstinate, obdurate priests. Therefore, when you know that a desecration of the Most Holy Communion is taking place in your parish, do not stand idly by. Once again, let us be mindful of the words of Saint James the Apostle: "Anyone [...] who knows the good he ought to do and does not do it, commits sin" (James 4:17). Therefore, I ask, I entreat, I beseech you again: Say categorically: "NO" to any kind of profanation of the Most Holy Eucharist. Please, do not scatter by your prodigal negligence, but gather by your restorative diligence.

Beloved Brothers and Sisters in our LORD Jesus Christ:

We must hope that the day will dawn when the profanation of the Most Holy Eucharist will finally end. We can attain this goal with the help of God and our determination, if only we persist in our courageous, constant and relentless efforts supported by our fervent prayers. The steadfastness of our attitude and the unwaveringness of our mind are absolutely

---

[111] N. P. Tanner, *vol. I*, op. cit., p. 562.
[112] Cf. ibid., p. 637.

crucial. Therefore, "do not be carried away by all kinds of strange teachings" (Hebrews 13:9a), and "avoid foolish and unlearned disputes, knowing that they generate strife. And a servant of the LORD must not quarrel, but be gentle to all, able to teach, patient, in humility correcting those who are in opposition, if God perhaps will grant them repentance, so that they may know the truth, and that they may come to their senses and escape the snare of the devil, having been taken captive by him to do his will" (2 Timothy 2:23–26). However, your gentleness, patience and humility should not deprive or weaken your firmness and steadfastness. Do not sow with such gentleness, patience and humility that you lose your firmness and steadfastness, because the profanation of the Most Holy Eucharist is a matter of life and death. If you act timidly, you will waste your time. "And let us not grow weary while doing good, for in due season we shall reap if we do not lose heart. Therefore, as we have opportunity, let us do good to all, especially to those who are of the household of faith" (Galatians 6:9–10); "make the most of the present opportunity, because the days are evil" (Ephesians 5:16). "Seek counsel from every wise man, and do not think lightly of any advice that can be useful. At all times bless the LORD God, and ask Him to make all your paths straight and to grant success to all your endeavors and plans" (Tobit 4:18–19a), "showing all good fidelity that [you] may adorn the doctrine of God, our Savior, in all things" (Titus 2:10). "Finally, be strong in the LORD and in the power of His might. Put on the whole armor of God so that you may be able to stand against the schemes of the devil. For our struggle is not against enemies of blood and flesh, but against the rulers, against the authorities, against the cosmic powers of this present darkness, against the spiritual forces of evil in the heavenly places. Therefore, take up the whole armor of God so that you may be able to withstand in the evil day, and having done all, to stand. Stand therefore, having girded your waist with truth, having put on the breastplate of righteousness, and having shod your feet with the preparation of the Gospel of peace; above all, taking the shield of faith with which you will be able to quench all the fiery darts of the wicked one. And take the helmet of salvation, and the sword of the Spirit, which is the word of God; praying always with all prayer and supplication in the Spirit, being watchful to this end with all perseverance and supplication for all the Saints, and for me, that utterance may be given to me, that I may open my mouth boldly to make known [the truth about the profanation of the Eucharist], for which I am an ambassador [for almost 20 years now]" (Ephesians 6:10–20a). Therefore, "stand fast in the LORD, Beloved" (Philippians 4:1), "in one spirit, with one mind, striving together for the [Eucharistic Jesus] [...], and not in any way terrified by your adversaries [...]. For to you it has been granted on behalf of Christ, not only to believe in Him, but also to suffer for His sake, having the same conflict which you saw in me and now hear is in me" (Philippians 1:27–30). I encourage you, "fill up in [your] flesh what is lacking in the afflictions of Christ, for the sake of His Body, which is the Church" (Colossians 1:24). By filling up in your flesh what is lacking in the afflictions of Christ, you will confirm that you are like Him, and being like Christ in His sufferings you will be like Him in His Glory.

The profanation of the Eucharist brings to tears those who believe in the real presence of Jesus Christ in this Most Holy Sacrament. With our eyes full of tears, we must do everything which is in our power to stop this sacrilegious practice in the heart of our Mother Church. May the encouragement of the Psalmist always sound not only in your ears, but first of all in your hearts, who says that "those who sow in tears will reap in joy"

(Psalm 126:5). What you must do now is struggle with this demonic abuse by your faith, prayer, words and actions; what you will reap at the final harvest will be – "the salvation of your souls" (1 Peter 1:9); "when Christ, who is our Life, appears, then you also will appear with Him in Glory" (Colossians 3:4). You are included in these words, if only you follow your faith confirmed with your good works. Therefore, as for now, "work out your own Salvation with fear and trembling, for it is God who is at work in you, both to will and to work for His good purpose" (Philippians 2:12–13). The LORD is sending "you out like sheep into the midst of wolves. Therefore, be wise as serpents and innocent as doves" (Matthew 10:16). "Now, may the God of Peace – who brought up our LORD Jesus from the dead, that great Shepherd of the sheep, through the Blood of the Everlasting Covenant – make you complete in every good work to do His will, working in you what is well pleasing in His sight, through Jesus Christ, to whom be Glory forever and ever. Amen. I appeal to you, Brothers [and Sisters], bear with the word of encouragement, [which] I have written to you in few words" (Hebrews 13:20–22). Act as "children of God without fault in the midst of a crooked and perverse generation, among whom you shine as lights in the world, holding fast the Word of Life, so that I may rejoice on the Day of Christ that I have not [written this book] in vain or labored in vain" (Philippians 2:15–16; cf. Deuteronomy 32:5c). I pray "that the God of our LORD Jesus Christ, the Father of Glory, may give to you the spirit of wisdom and revelation in the knowledge of Him" (Ephesians 1:17), then at the time of trial, it will not be "you who [will] speak, but the Spirit of your Father [will speak] in you" (Matthew 10:20), "for the Holy Spirit will teach you in that very hour what you ought to say" (Luke 12:12). Because our Divine Master assures you, saying: "I will give you a mouth and wisdom which all your adversaries will not be able to contradict or resist" (Luke 21:15). Therefore, on your part, "do not grow weary in doing good" (2 Thessalonians 3:13), "but grow in the grace and knowledge of our LORD and Savior Jesus Christ" (2 Peter 3:18a). "By your endurance you will gain your souls" (Luke 21:19). "Faithful is He who calls you, and He also will do it" (1 Thessalonians 5:24), when He, "the God of Peace, will crush satan under your feet shortly" (Romans 16:20a). Then, at the sunset of your life, you will exclaim together with Saint Paul the Apostle: "I have fought the good fight, I have finished the race, I have kept the faith. Finally, there is laid up for me the crown of righteousness, which the LORD, the Righteous Judge, will give to me on that Day, and not to me only, but also to all who have loved His appearing" (2 Timothy 4:7–8). Let everyone know "your love and faith which you have toward the LORD Jesus ..." (Philemon 5), and may your loyal service in the Roman-Catholic Church be a pleasant offering to the Glory of God; may it become "the fragrance of your good ointments, [and] your name [be] perfume poured forth" (Song of Solomon 1:3a) before the Throne of the Almighty God for eternal memory when "you will rise for your reward at the end of the days" (Daniel 12:13b).

In my final words addressed to you, Brothers and Sisters, I ask you to turn your minds and hearts to Mary, the Most Blessed Mother of our LORD Jesus Christ, who always accompanies Her Most Beloved Son. We read in the Gospel of Saint Luke that at the time of the presentation of our LORD in the Jerusalem Temple, the Prophet Simeon, inspired by the Holy Spirit, came into the temple (cf. Luke 2:27a), "and when the parents brought in the Child Jesus, to do for Him according to the custom of the Law, he took Him up in his arms and blessed God ... [...]. Then, Simeon blessed them, and said to Mary His Mother, 'Behold, this Child is destined for the fall and rising of many in Israel, and for a sign that will be opposed, and You Yourself will be pierced with a sword so that the thoughts of many hearts may be revealed'" (Luke 2:27b–28.34–35). This prophecy fulfilled itself in the life of Mary when She suffered together with Her suffering Son during His Passion, and especially when She stood at the foot of His Cross at Golgotha. However, the Mother of God is also present at any Celebration of the Eucharistic Sacrifice, inasmuch as She never parts from Her Son. And today, Her soul is being pierced with a sword over and over again when the Most Precious Eucharistic Blood of Her Beloved Son is being desecrated. Therefore, whenever we think about the profanation of the Eucharistic LORD, let us never forget about His Sorrowful Mother, but turn the thoughts of our hearts to Her who is always perfectly united with Her Son, sharing and taking His sufferings as Her own.

Brothers and Sisters, please, "listen to my appeal, be of one mind, live in peace, and the God of Love and Peace will be with you" (2 Corinthians 13:11c.d). "The Grace of the LORD Jesus Christ, and the Love of God, and the Communion of the Holy Spirit be with you all. Amen" (2 Corinthians 13:13).

"It is time for You to act, O LORD, for they have regarded Your Law as void" (Psalm 119:126). LORD, if You do not like what I have delivered in this book, may it be forever forgotten, but if You are pleased with its message, then "may the words of my mouth and the thoughts of my heart win favor in Your sight, O LORD, my Rock and my Redeemer" (Psalm 19:15); may the words of this book go out through all the earth; may they reach to the ends of the world (cf. Psalm 19:5a; Romans 10:18c); may they resound "from the rising of the sun, even to its setting" (Malachi 1:11a; cf. Psalm 50:1; 113:3), and may they pierce the minds and hearts of the people, Your People. AMEN.

On Ash Wednesday 2015

BIBLIOGRAPHY

Code of Canon Law. Latin–English Edition. Translation prepared under the auspices of the Canon Law Society of America (Washington, D.C. 1983)

Cogan, P. J., *The Canon Law Digest, vol. XIV* (Washington, D.C. 2012)

Cross, F. L. – Livingstone, E. A., The Oxford Dictionary of the Christian Church (Oxford 1993)

General Instruction of the Roman Missal (Washington, D.C. 2003)

Gove, P. B., Webster's Third New International Dictionary of the English Language Unabridged (Springfield, Massachusetts 1993)

Handford, S. A. – Herberg, M., Langenscheidt's Pocket Latin Dictionary (Berlin – Munich 1966)

Instruction on the Eucharist *Redemptionis Sacramentum*: On Certain Matters to Be Observed or to Be Avoided Regarding the Most Holy Eucharist (Washington, D.C. 2004)

Kowalska, M. F., *Diary* (Stockbridge, Massachusetts 2003)

Morwood, J., The Pocket Oxford Latin Dictionary (Oxford 1995)

Simpson, D. P., Cassell's Latin Dictionary (New York 1968)

Tanner, N. P., *Decrees of the Ecumenical Councils, vol. I–II* (London–Washington, D.C. 1990)

The Liturgy of the Hours, vol. I–IV (New York 1975–1976)

The New American Bible (New York 1970)

The Roman Missal (New Jersey 2011)

This Holy and Living Sacrifice: Directory for the Celebration and Reception of Communion under Both Kinds (Washington, D.C. 1985)

CPSIA information can be obtained at www.ICGtesting.com
Printed in the USA
BVOW07s1516310315

394117BV00002B/3/P